# POINT AND SHOOT

## A Railway Photographic Memoir

### Volume One
### Locomotives on shed

### TED READING

First published 2010
FINIAL PUBLISHING

ISBN 978-1-900467-45-2

Produced by Finial Publishing
15 Abingdon Drive, Caversham Park, Reading, RG4 6SA
Telephone: 01189-484103
Email: mail@finial.co.uk

Printed by Henry Ling Ltd, The Dorset Press, Dorchester, Dorset, DT1 1HD
Telephone: 01305 251066
www.henryling.co.uk

# DEDICATION

## IRIS READING

For all Iris's help with this project and for much much more.

Iris hides behind the Kodak 44A camera of Paul Wells, one of the few photographic relics remaining of the 1960s.

## FRANK ASKEY (1916 - 1996)

Without whose help and encouragement little in the way of photography would have been achieved, and thus no book would ever have been published.
Born in Australia from Italian descent and moved to Scotland prior to the Second World War in which he served in the Army. Married shortly after the war, having two children and worked in the family business, the Askey wafer biscuit concern at Kensal Green, London, then Aylesbury.

# THE AUTHOR'S TALE

Firstly, many thanks for buying my book, the first, hopefully, of a short series of photographic endeavours covering a twenty year span from the 1960s. I hope you will forgive my continual reference to motorcycles, this is an indulgence on my part but it fits in with the period covered by this book.

For want of a better year to start an introduction 1988 will do. I had rejoined the real working world after spending five years travelling up and down the countryside photographing railways whilst under the guise of working for a car leasing company.

My workmate and long time friend Paul Wells, then sadly died following a car accident and with his going a link with the past was lost. Over many years we had shared an interest in railways and motorcycles.

My enthusiasm over railways, well trainspotting, goes way back to the fifties. Starting work in 1961 as a laboratory assistant in the foundry trade my elder brother's hand-me-down moped came my way. This gave rise to a greater interest in motorbikes, eventually my only contact with railways being yearly 'lads day out' to Barry locomotive dump with long time chums Paul, Peter Askey and John Durrant. On meeting

Ted, Peter, John and Paul,
Barry Dump, December 1975.

my Iris even the bikes took a bit of a back seat. Following on from a serious industrial accident in 1977 - I fell through the foundry roof - my interest in railways was reborn. In need of some drastic therapy, the body parts were not working too well, Iris encouraged me to get out and about, so eventually I wandered off photographing trains.

With interest redoubled more 'lads day outs' were organised revisiting old haunts and photographing, even then, a fast changing general railway scene.

These excursions proved shortlived as Paul loved driving but it was of the kind that could best be described as 'interesting'. He always managed to get into one scrape or another and eventually Peter and John thought the better of it, the final straw being a high speed dash down a Welsh mountain side.

However, I must have been of sterner stuff and carried on until Paul's untimely death and that really was an end to it. Not much fun by yourself.

There was some compensations as the family grew up - much to Iris and the children's dismay our holiday destinations always seemed to include a railway backdrop.

When, at their age back in the 1950s, any holiday with railway involvement, however tenuous, was looked upon by myself with great enthusiasm.

In early 1954, at the age of nine, the family moved to Greenford, West London, and thus on starting a new school one 'Buster', aka, Clive Featherstone, soon came my way. Buster was exciting, a leader of men, well of me at least. But for all the world we were two scruffy urchins that had by the age of ten or thereabouts mastered travelling around London and could navigate the Underground without adult assistance of any kind.

We were trainspotters, and for us our second home was Southall railway bridge spanning the former GW mainline out of Paddington.

Ted and Buster, Shelley Close,
Greenford c. 1955

By early 1959 Buster had decided it was time to spread our wings and that our meagre collection of train numbers would be dramatically increased by launching a full assault on the capital's loco sheds.

No easy prospect, so with pounding heart Willesden was the first attempted and over the Summer, armed with our London Transport Twin Rovers, we were pretty well chucked out, thrown out and ordered out of the Capital's loco sheds. Some of these establishments were near impregnable but by year's end we had bunked all that London had to offer, some many times over.

Ted, Feltham loco shed, December 1960, taken by Buster.

At some stage of the proceedings we both acquired pushbikes. Whilst Buster built up a state of the art Claud Butler lightweight racing job my dad did me proud by acquiring a gentleman's maroon Rudge. The thing weighed a ton, rod brakes, fully enclosed rear chain guard and, of course, a Sturmy Archer three speed gearing. For me a total embarrassment but you could, if money was short, just about heave it around London.

Train spotting opened our horizons with occasional train trips on our own as well as days out with Buster's parents and our own annual family holidays to Brighton. These were the highlights of a year, only somewhat blighted by the fact that Buster discovered I was half blind.

Not so good for a trainspotter who seemingly could not spot numbers unless he fell over the engine. This was something of a liability to the furtive spotter, not that I had realised it. As my eyesight seemingly deteriorated I gravitated to the front of the classroom and struggled to avoid the embarrassment and humiliating ridicule from classmates on having to wear National Health issue goggles. John Lennon came too late for me.

1960 dawned and disaster for Teddy.

Buster lost interest. Model Railways had taken him over and it wasn't long before his bedroom disappeared under layers of hardboard all supported by a Forth bridge style erection of 'two by one' timber. Worse was to follow, Buster left school and took up an engineering apprenticeship at Napiers, in Acton Vale, the manufacturer of Deltic engines.

Train spotting classmates were now thin on the ground as even Terry Bennet, best known as Ben, who you will come across if you read my next book, went off to join British Railways at West Ealing signal box.

Drastic measures were called for, the only other option being to join a club. Previously we had all frowned on this as we thought trainspotters clubs were for mummies boys, school cap, blazers, badges and all that sort of thing.

But by late 1960 I had joined The Home Counties Railway Club known to all as the 'Homo's'. Trips with the 'Homo's' were a real eye opener. We were the boys equivalent of St Trinians. For hockey sticks read notebooks and biros and you get the picture, I don't think the organisers ever had a permit between them

Clive 'Buster' Featherstone, Shelley Close, Greenford 1961.

Whilst I carried on as before, Buster, even at school, was already toying with girls' affections and on starting work soon acquired a 650cc BSA Super Rocket.

But one last trip with Buster, a pushbike ride to Feltham Loco in late 1960, was to have a great impression on me and it wasn't his mum's cheese and cucumber sandwiches.

Buster, for the first time, toted a camera, or more a camera shaped object. It was cheap. It was plastic It took pictures.

Our family had a camera. It was tatty old metal Box Brownie. We took it on holidays. Sometimes pictures would be seen, but only dad ever loaded film into the thing. Sometimes nothing ever came out.

Photographs, so I thought, were for the wealthy. We did 'snaps' and 'snapping' trains hadn't really entered Teddy's head.

But Buster's snaps at Feltham made a great impression at school, most lads in those days didn't own cameras. Well not at our school, Brentside Secondary Modern Boys. Whilst the dog-eared copy of 'Lady Chatterlies Lover' did the rounds, pictures of trains or anything else were rarely seen.

The impact on me was immediate. The Box Brownie was commandeered, pocket money scraped together for a roll of Kodak 620 size film from Boots the Chemist and by the beginning of 1961 I was on my way to Old Oak Common. Mother was concerned, she seemed to view the camera as a family heirloom, dad, I think was glad to see the back of it. Back to Boots for processing and being much impressed would proudly show my snaps at school to anyone who would look at them. One young lad, Peter Askey, two years below me, showed an interest as both he and his dad, Frank, were keen on photography.

It wasn't long before introductions were made to the Askey family and Frank, Peter's father, was showing us the mysterious ways of darkroom lore.

When twenty pounds cash came my way and with very little in the way of forethought, or even consulting Frank, I rushed round to Boots and purchased a cheap 127 size plastic Kodak 44A camera box set. It even had a plastic clip on flash. On proudly showing my purchase to Frank and Peter they needless to say were reduced to tears.

Home Counties Club trips accounted for the rest of the money so I had to put up with the camera. Still on a good sunny day the old 44A being of a largish 127 format could produce, for a beginner, a decent result. That is until the sun went in, then it was game over.

On joining the working world I purchased some stylish heavy black-framed glasses then saved up for a camera, a 35mm Kodak Retinette 1A. Peter, on the other hand, had finally managed to prize Frank's camera away from him, a 120 size bellows Kershaw with Taylor Hobson lens, a great all British camera. This he used until the day he purchased a Minolta A5, a 35mm rangefinder jobby. Perhaps not so good but a lot cheaper to run. My Retinette 1A was eventually traded in for a Russian Fed-2, the word in the photographic magazines being, for the price, it had an excellent lens.

Ted will ill-fated Zenith and Mamiyaflex, Eastleigh loco shed, 25th August 1963.

I think that it did, but the rest wasn't quite up to it. Mine started suffering from a focal plane shutter problem giving uneven exposure so it had to go. So thanks to the joys of hire purchase I went up in the world with a 120 size Mamiyaflex twin lens reflex. Brilliant though this camera was I was for ever running out of film and in those days even if you found a chemist shop open on a Sunday, they couldn't sell you a film. Even if you begged. A Russian Zenith SLR was purchased as a back up, not the world's best buy and dropping it on the floor didn't help, so both went for a 35mm Minolta SR1 single lens reflex.

However during this period events were rapidly overtaking us. Back in the fifties stored and dumped engines were relatively unknown other than at, as I recall, Nine Elms shed and at various locomotive works.

But by 1962 it all started to change. Willesden suddenly had two 'Princess' Pacifics in store which I couldn't believe. But this was a prelude of things to come as we began to witness the demise of

Paul Wells, Swindon Works,
5th July 1964.

steam. As the year ticked by every shed seemed to contain rapidly increasing numbers of withdrawn locos, the 'Kings' had gone by year's end and large swathes of Southern types went at a stroke.

The sudden demise of steam took us by surprise and as the number of withdrawn locos increased so did our of photographing of them. Also, at that age there were other things in life to interest us as well as railways. Worse still a total bias developed for the Western and Southern regions. It seemed better to photograph endless lines of dumped pannier tanks than to perhaps wander eastwards to record the demise of the 'other' regions. Even nature started to conspire against us, as trainspotters it was of no concern what the weather was doing but with photography in mind complete trips could be marred by dull, wet, unforgiving weather. On the transport front Peter had finally convinced mum and dad on the necessity of having a motorbike and by then we had met up with Paul and John, both two wheeled railway enthusiasts.

Paul was also keen on photography, yet another Kodak 44A.

Looking back my adventures with the 'Homo's' only lasted for just over a year. However they offered a varied itinerary even if, on occasions, there was little time to even get the camera out of its case. The four of us then continued shed bashing by train or motorbike and even occasionally with permits. As photography took preference things were done at a more leisurely pace even if, as the book title suggests, very much on the basis of 'point and shoot'. My picture taking spanned little more than four years. I was seventeen by the time I had progressed to the Mamiyaflex from the Box Brownie and was little over nineteen by the time it was all over.

To sum up, a visit to Kings Cross Loco during the Summer of 1963 toting the Mamiflex produced a single A3, when last visited three years previous when Teddy was in full trainspotting mode it was a full house.

Although the demise of the steam locomotive caused me great sadness I am glad to have been around to witness some part of it. Whether the British Railways Modernisation plan had been implemented or not time was up for us and we had all moved on.

By the time of my roof escapade in 1977 when a somewhat incapacitated Teddy took to the trains again, the railways were in their 'blue' period, train numbers were all TOPS, and the steam engine was history.

Peter Askey, Old Oak Common, 24th January 1965.

# FROM SILVER HALIDES TO PIXELS

On reflection this book owes a lot to Frank Askey. Although a amateur photographer he was very professional in his outlook and I doubt I would have progressed much past the box camera stage without him. Another factor was that unable to afford better photographic equipment on my wages my parents would sign hire purchase agreements on my behalf.

Buying my first 35mm camera I initially used Ilford HP3 400ASA film but through the Summer of 1962, I underwent a photographic learning curve. This was not a good time for doing this. Buying film in bulk was a sound option, but ex-MOD film was not such a good idea nor was trying high speed films. All generally gave poor, or in a few cases, disastrous results. Eventually I settled down to 125ASA FP3 and a second hand Weston exposure meter was purchased replacing a simple plastic dial-up device. Processing was done round at the Askey's home in the kitchen, films were loaded up in the dark under the stairs. Fine grain developers Promicrol and Microdol were used with high speed fixers which greatly reduced processing times. Printing pictures was exceedingly time consuming and required great skill, thus developing films then outstripped printing and both Peter and myelf eventually built up huge backlog of negatives. These were then initially stored in a haphazard way and it was not until later that all the negatives were placed into albums. By then some of the early ones had gone missing, for example very few Midland region negatives survive prior to 1963.

Two house moves, and some forty years later my eldest son presented me with a stand alone 35mm scanner/printer. Actually he didn't present it to me, he purchased it on a whim and then sold it to me knowing I had an interest in digital scanning. He was not wrong. However within six months the retail price had dropped by fifty quid, then another fifty and within another six months it vanished off the radar screen. Such is technology. My initial efforts showed some promise but attempting BW printing on a colour printer has its limitations. But by trial and error and using professional photographic papers reasonable results were produced. At this stage there was no thought of a book but two factors then came together which not only improved print quality but put the thoughts of a book in my mind.

Elder son then took pity and gave us a lap top. However to fully explain its workings we had to tie him to a chair to stop him escaping. Shortly after this Iris signed me up for a one day course on digital imaging. This introduced me to Picasa, a free download from Google, and it has to be said I never looked back, even purchasing another scanner catering for large format negatives. At that stage the old enlarger, lenses etc finally came down from the attic and went to the car boot.

Then in 2008 events took a dramatic turn, a railway package holiday to the Hartz mountains introduced us to one fellow traveller John Villers, a publisher of books.

Not only a publisher of books, but one with a great interest in railways who lives in striking distance of home. Approaching John about doing a book he agreed to take on the project, for that is what it has been. Without his help and encouragement this book would never have happened and I would not have spent the past few years living under the stairs with two scanners and a lap top in a state of mortal fear waiting for a systems crash. I have even became conversant with a memory stick. Forty years on and I'm back under the stairs again simply because we live in a very small house, but at least with the new technology I have light.

Setting the book up picture wise has taken considerable time and at this stage I must thank Peter for allowing me the use of his own negative collection not only for this book but, should it see the light of day, the next, 'Steam on the Move'. On Paul's death I inherited his negative collection so it pleases me to include some of his 44A Plastic camera shots. At the time Paul had his own priorities, and that was buying a Honda 250 and not a better camera.

My thanks go to Clive 'Buster' Featherstone for helping me get some order into the events of fifty years past and passing a critical eye over my ramblings and also to Neville Bridger of Nevis Books for filling my attic with countless railway journals of the 1960s so that I may appear more knowledgeable than what I really am.

I have to say that the pictorial quality is more old approach than the 'new approach' of railway photography in the mid 1960s, but although all the negatives have been digitally scanned, other than negative imperfections removed, what you see is what you get. Of technical interest 35mm negs have been scanned at 2400dpi and 120 size at 1200dpi.

## PHOTOGRAPHIC DISASTERS!

*UNDER MY
STAIRS BOOKS*

# AUTHOR'S NOTE

The purchaser of my book may find the subject matter somewhat out of order. The first two parts, Western and Southern steam are laid out in order of Locomotive Motive Power Depots whilst the remainder, Midland Steam, Diesels, and Withdrawn Locomotives are in locomotive class order. The reason for this is that my interest at the time was mainly for the Western and Southern Regions. The Midland Region was generally ignored added to the fact that many varied location shots on this region have sadly gone missing. The 'Dumped and Derelict' part was always planned to be in locomotive class order, but on compiling the Midland Steam and Diesels parts it rapidly became apparent at the majority of photographs were taken at the same locations.

Whatever, I trust that you will enjoy my book as much as I have had enjoyment in compiling it. As I am now myself in the 'dumped and derelict' part of life, I presume you to be in a similar state of affairs to purchase it. Therefore I trust you will be around for Volume Two, so long as I'm about to do it!

## OLD OAK COMMON

Plate 1.  Nos.92209, 5070 *Sir Daniel Gooch*, 4701  6th September 1963   Mamiya C22

Plate 2.  Pannier Tanks                              19th May 1963                              Mamiya C22

One of the first loco depots that Buster and I were uninvited to was Old Oak Common. This  became my 'home from home' for the next few years and once inside was never challenged. Old Oak was huge with four 65ft electrically driven wooden covered turntables under one roof,  they were a joy to stand on or even erect your tripod and camera and go for a spin. It was the prototype of a roundhouse design by Churchward and was built in 1906, eight were built but none to the size of Old Oak Common.

# OLD OAK COMMON

Plate 3.  No.6000 *King George V*          6th October 1962          Fed-2

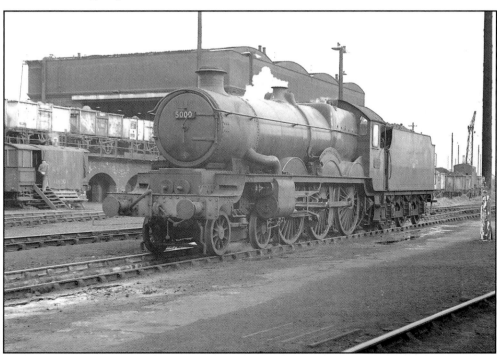

Plate 4.  No.5000 *Launceston Castle*          28th October 1962          Fed-2

Visits in the late '50s could manage well over one hundred steam locos the only diesels being a line of shunters parked up by the works. By 1962 the introduction of main line diesels was well established with steam in decline but within a year of closure around fifty locos could be seen in steam. Plate 1 shows the turntable drive control. No.5070 is having work done to her safety valve.

Plate 5. No.4089 *Donnington Castle*          6th October 1962                    Fed-2

Plate 6. No.5081 *Lockheed Hudson*          29th September 1962                 Fed-2

Plate 2 shows the less glamorous side to loco working, pannier tanks resting between empty carriage duties, a mainstay at Old Oak until replaced by Type 2 diesel hydraulics brought up from the West Country in 1962. Old Oak's top link locos were the 'Kings' but as early as 1959 'The Bristolian' was to become diesel hauled. West Country expresses were the next to go and by 1961 the 'Kings' were working the South Wales and Wolverhampton expresses only, finally being reduced just to the Wolverhampton service and this would be their swansong.

Plate 7. No.4950 *Patshull Hall*          6th October 1962          Fed-2

Plate 8. No.4971 *Stanway Hall*          12th August 1962          Fed -2

In September 1962 the Wolverhampton service was officially dieselised but the 'Kings' continued substituting for diesel failures until the end of the year. In Plate 3, 'King' No.6000 stands in front of the duty roster board, but by this date only she and classmates Nos.6005/11/18 remained working. Towards the end of 1962 Nos.6000/18 worked various special trains to South Wales and Nos.6000/5/11 the October Newbury race day specials, the last time three 'Kings' were to be seen at Paddington station together.

Plate 9. No.2836          12th October 1963                    Mamiya C22

Plate 10. No.4703                    16th June 1963                    Mamiya C22

'Castles' were always a mainstay at Old Oak and by the end of the 1950s nearly forty were allocated to Old Oak but by 1963 their last main line duties were the Hereford and Worcester expresses. Plate 4 shows No.5000 with the giant coaling plant and water tank forming a magnificent backdrop. I love the grounded 'Toad' brake van, no doubt in use for coaling plant men to have a brew. Plate 6 shows No.5081 which was renamed *Lockheed Hudson* during the Second World War after a serving RAF aircraft. This nameplate mystified me as

# OLD OAK COMMON

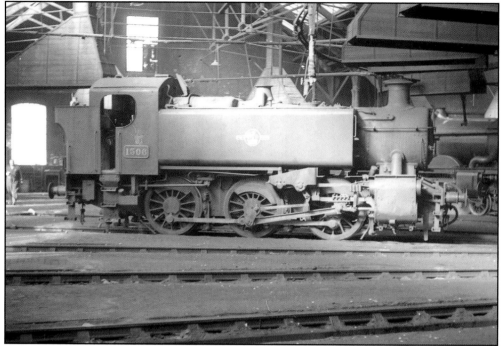

Plate 11. No.1506          29th September 1962          Fed-2

Plate 12. No.9498          16th August 1964          Minolta SR1

The 'Halls' were 'maids of all work' and Plate 7 shows No.4950 alongside the 1950s amenities block, the photograph being dated by the car, whilst No.4971 (Plate 8) stands in the shed yards with a peep view of a old wooden private owner wagon. Although a 'Top Link' depot, freight locos such as '28xx', LMS '8Fs', and BR Standard '9Fs' were regularly seen, and the entire '47xx' class were allocated and mostly withdrawn from Old Oak. Towards the end of steam strangers became commonplace notably 'Manor' and '45xx' Prairie tanks.

Plate 13.  No.9707                    29th September 1962                    Fed-2

Plate 14.  No.80105                    29th July 1962                    Kodak Retinette 1A

Large numbers of panniers were always present including the '57xx' condensing tanks built for working the London Transport running lines between Paddington and Smithfield market. Some of these condensing tanks retained their links with the past, Nos.9703/9 retaining 'GWR' and No.9710 the GWR button on their tank sides to the end. Between June and October 1962 Old Oak played guest to a dozen displaced Tilbury line BR Standard class '4MT' tanks. No.80105 was one such example and was transferred away to North Wales by August 1962.

Plate 15.  No.1622                    2nd December 1962                    Fed-2

A 61xx Prairie tank on Slough depot,
July 1963.

Plate 16.  No.7308        14th July 1963        Mamiya C22

Slough, to me, was for a 'B' depot somewhat on the small size and on my first visit in the Summer of 1959 was all '61xx' Prairie tanks, in fact some twenty were allocated there. The newly introduced DMUs were stabled across the Windsor branch running lines in a dilapidated carriage shed which was soon demolished, or fell down! The '14xx' tanks departed in the early 1960s and much to my surprise two '16xx' panniers arrived from the Summer of 1962 which were then withdrawn when the shed closed in June 1964.

Plate 17.  No.6125                    5th April 1964                    Mamiya C22

Plate 18.  Nos.6110 & 6160            25th July 1964                    Minolta SR1

Southall was, as a trainspotter, my second home through the mid to late 1950s, and more amazing was that we never got into the depot until the Summer of 1959 and only then with a permit. The shed had been rebuilt in the early 1950s with a north light pattern roof and Plate 16 shows No.7308, not a common class at Southall, waiting to come off shed by the original coaler which had been retained as the water tank formed the roof. The base of the original water softener can be seen on the left of No.7308 with the new one behind.

Plate 19.  No.4700                    16th September 1962                    Fed-2

Plate 20.  No.6841 *Marlas Grange*          29th September 1962          Fed-2

The replacement coaling plant was more primitive than what it replaced, a hoist and tub affair situated at the rear of the shed. Old Great Western railcars, either maroon or blood and custard, were always present during the 1950s and could regularly be seen alongside the depot by the main line or parked up on the shed head shunt. New DMU stock started appearing in 1959 and the old railcars had gone by early 1961.

Plate 21.  No.4914 *Cranmore Hall*　　　　　14th July 1963　　　　　Mamiya C22

Plate 22.  No.3801　　　　　16th September 1962　　　　　Fed-2

Despite being primarily a freight depot a good variety of locos could always be seen, with 'Halls' and 'Granges' mixed in with the ubiquitous panniers and, despite the dieselisation of the Paddington local services, the '61xx' Prairie tanks. Of the panniers No.8731 (Plate 24) was Southall's last example of the original build '57xx' class, she was withdrawn in July 1962. Other than the DMUs Southall remained a steam depot, the only other diesels being shunters which arrived in 1960.

Plate 23.  No.5569                    5th April 1964                    Mamiya C22

Plate 24.  No.8731                    12th December 1961                    Kodak Retinette 1A

By the time of my first visit freight workings were in the hands of Great Western '28xx', '47xx' and 'WD' 2-8-0's. In Plate 22 No.3801 graces an empty shed yard alongside the Foreman's office The following year, 1960, BR Standard '9Fs' were introduced and over the next few years the 'WD' types faded away and from 1963 onwards more was seen of LMS '8Fs' although none were ever allocated there. Plate 25 shows a local 'WD' with the coaler in the background now assisted by a grab mounted crane and Plate 26 a visiting '9F' in

Plate 25. No.90356            29th September 1962            Fed-2

Plate 26. No.92236            7th July 1964            Minolta SR1

Over the years the numbers of locomotives in steam never diminished and added variety was to be had by the allocation of '45xx' light Prairie tanks at the end of 1963 (Plate 23), and even four 'Castles', a class that rarely graced Southall, found their way there during the Summer of 1964, not that I ever saw much of them in steam. All were withdrawn within a few months.

Plate 27. Front Ends           4th February 1962           Kodak Retinette 1A

Plate 28. No.7829 *Ramsbury Manor*        12th July 1964         Minolta SR1

By June 1959 a new diesel depot had been opened for DMU stock which soon displaced the '61xx' Prairie tanks from the outer London suburban services. The steam depot was a nine road affair mostly dead ended with a turntable immediately outside which was once incorporated within the shed building. Two large water tanks were situated alongside the Newbury running lines, resulting in the coaler not requiring a water tank for a roof, which was unusual for the Great Western.

# READING

Plate 29.  No.2874                    2nd December 1962                    Fed-2

Plate 30.  No.6107                    12th July 1964                    Minolta SR1

The smoky interior revealed in Plate 27 shows 'Castle' No.5067 one of several allocated here over the years and Plate 28 depicts 'Manor' No.7829 one of six allocated to Reading from 1962 onwards. 'Manors' had been, up to that time, very rare birds in the London division and were to become regular performers on the Reading to Redhill service as late as 1964. No.7829 hauled the last scheduled steam service from Reading to Redhill on 1st January 1965.

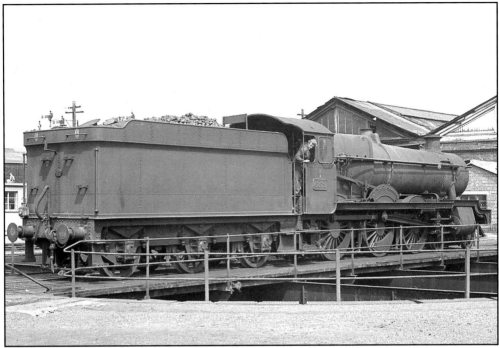

Plate 31. No.6872 *Crawley Grange*        19th July 1964        Minolta SR1

Plate 32. No.7236        30th September 1962        Fed-2

'Granges' were never overabundant at Reading, but several were allocated from September 1962 onwards. No.6872,positioned on the under-girder turntable, was not an allocated loco but a stranger. Much more unusual was '72xx' heavy tank No.7236 stationed by the turntable on a very wet and misty day. Such was their rarity that three months earlier another had been noted on shed in the railway press having worked empty passenger stock.

# DIDCOT

Plate 33.  No.6112                          19th July 1964                          Minolta SR1

Plate 34.  No.8720                          19th July 1964                          Minolta SR1

This shed was one of nine built by the Great Western under the Government Loan Act between 1929 to 1934 to combat high unemployment during the depression. Construction was of brick, steel and corrugated asbestos. First visited early in 1961 it seemed a home for 'Halls', '28xx', and '61xx' Prairie tanks but for a London division depot, interestingly also '43xx' Moguls. From 1962 onwards 'Counties' and 'Granges' put in appearances and to add a bit of glamour, unlike today's Didcot, even a 'Castle' now and again.

Plate 35. No.3859          19th July 1964          Minolta SR1

Plate 36. No.1015 *County of Gloucester*          30th September 1962          Fed-2

With six visits over three years No.8720 in Plate 34 holds something of a record of being on shed on all six occasions, this particular photo being the last such time. The four 'Counties' allocated there during 1962 seem to make grim reading for although employed on a variety of duties they appeared to have been in poor mechanical condition. Hence No.1015 is undergoing some attention which probably got nowhere as it was withdrawn the following month.

Plate 37.  Nos.6923 *Croxteth Hall* & 9653          19th July 1964          Minolta SR1

Plate 38.  No.5089 *Westminster Abbey*          3rd June 1963          Mamiya C22

The shed was of timber construction and old enough to accommodate broad gauge engines. On my first visit it seemed to be on the verge of instant collapse but it survived another three years before demolition. Oxford was an interesting location and there was always a wide variety of locos from other regions, more so when the 'Pines Express' was diverted through in 1963. Pulling out of the shed yard is No.5089 to relieve No.34103 which had just been brought off a train from the south.

Plate 39.  No.4921 *Eaton Hall*                     26th August 1962                     P Askey - Kershaw

Plate 40.  No.4704                     26th August 1962                     P Askey - Kershaw

Excursions to Bristol generally followed on from a tour around Swindon and by then usually with no film stock left. At least on one occasion Peter managed some discipline, and on 26th August 1962 near seventy locos were on shed including, inside the now gloomy depot, saddle tank No.1365 and pannier tank No.6408 as stationary boiler. Alongside the coaler 'Hall' No.4921 takes on water but is withdrawn the following month, whilst No.4704 is outside the twin turntable shed building.

# SWINDON

Plate 41.  No.5063 *Earl Baldwin*          26th August 1962                    Fed-2

Plate 42.  No.4949 *Packwood Hall*          14th January 1962          Kodak Retinette 1A

On my first visit to Swindon in June 1959 the depot seemed to hold just about all the loco types I never came across, including, one this occasion *City of Truro*. It was rumoured that the stock shed, which was set back from the loco shed alongside the Swindon to Gloucester main line, held long withdrawn Prairie tanks. If it did we were to be denied, the building was locked.

Plate 43.  No.4989 *Cherwell Hall*          26th August 1962          Fed-2

Plate 44.  No.82001          26th August 1962          Fed-2

The loco depot itself consisted of a straight shed running into a roundhouse with a later-build roundhouse alongside. On the occasion of our visit in August 1962 this roundhouse was near empty with little company for BR Standard class '3MT' tank No.82001. Two roads of the straight shed had been partitioned off as the diesel 'Experimental Shed', well that's what we were told. Entry was barred but looking through the windows we saw a couple of new build railbuses. Experimental, but hardly exciting.

# SWINDON

Plate 45. No.W33/38W                    16th December 1962                    Fed-2

Plate 46. No.5815                       14th January 1962                    Kodak  Retinette 1A

Plate 41 shows the coaler as a backdrop to 'Castle' No.5063, whist Plate 45 views the coaler and long shed from the other side. It is worth recording here No.5815 was withdrawn back in April 1961 but remained a long term resident outside the stock shed until scrapped in June 1964. I always wondered if it was a preservation project. Also note the undulating roof line of a newly constructed railway works building which was still in existence in the 1980s.

Plate 47.  No.3605  22nd September 1962  P Askey - Minolta A5

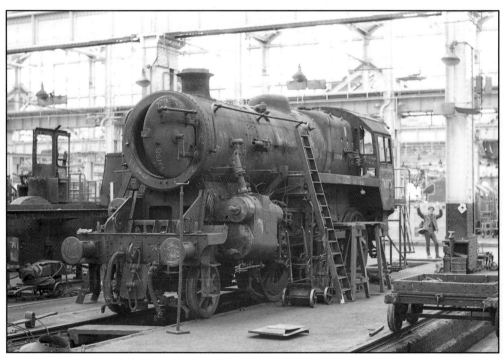

Plate 48.  No.76075  5th July 1964  Minolta SR1

Swindon Works 'A' Shop was for this trainspotter the place to be. A cathedral to steam, a massive open glazed high roofed building with a light airy feel to it. The locomotive works area itself formed only a part of this huge manufacturing complex, no wonder, on arriving at Swindon station you realised this was a railway town. These pictures give some account as to the openness of the works, plus a preponderance of ladders a basic requirement for the job in hand. In the bottom picture I was surprised to see chum Paul waving to the camera, not a done thing, which if the photo had been printed forty five years ago, would not have best pleased me.

Plate 49. No.92220 *Evening Star*      2nd February 1964      Mamiya C22

Plate 50. No. 7010 *Avondale Castle*      26th August 1962      Fed-2

At this time 'Castle' class locos were still having double chimneys fitted and the last locomotive actually repaired here was 'Castle' No.4079 in February 1965. The Works yard ran along the Bristol to Swindon main line, passing erecting and boiler shop, iron foundry and fitting/machine shops. These pictures depict '9F' No.92220 *Evening Star* awaiting attention and 'Castle' No.7010, ex-works, with 'A' Shop forming an imposing background.

Plate 51. No.6018 *King Henry VI*        26th May 1963        Mamiya C22

Plate 52. No.7929 *Wkye Hall*        16th December 1962        Fed-2

To the passing train passenger positioning 'King' No.6018 alongside the main line might have set the scene for an era recently gone. One of the last to be withdrawn in December 1962 and then called to Swindon Works in early 1963 and then on to Tyseley to prepare her for the SLS 'Last King' run on the 28th April 1963. This ran from Birmingham and return pulling twelve coaches at 440 tons gross, topping 90mph down Denham Bank, travelling via the Greenford loop and stopping at Southall and Swindon.

Plate 53.  No.7248                    11th November 1962                    Fed-2

Plate 54.  No.73034                    8th November 1964                    Minolta SR1

The weighbridge was positioned just along from the main works and 'Modified Hall' No.7929 poses outside in Plate 52. Positioned around the works over-girder turntable are Nos.7248 and 73034. Our railway enthusiasts in the top photo, look professional, while one totes a 35mm single lens reflex, for 1962 a cool piece of kit, his mate seemingly carries all the gear.

# SWINDON WORKS

Generally ignored, Swindon Works shunters are still steam but gone are the days of obscure South Wales tanks doing the job. Both these pictures feature '57xx' pannier tanks, both were withdrawn and within months meet the scrap man. No.7756 is parked in the Works yard with the driving wheels from *The Lord of the Isles* for company - did they survive or were they scrapped? The bottom photo has No.7799 with the works as a backdrop and the reception shed, or the barn as it was known, on the left of the photo with the weighbridge behind.

Plate 57. No.6955 *Lydcott Hall*        19th July 1964        Minolta SR1

Plate 58. No.3739        19th July 1964        Minolta SR1

Westbury was somewhat off the beaten track and only visited on a few occasions. On this particular visit twenty locos were on shed with a handful of diesel shunters. 'Hall' No.6955 stands outside the shed alongside the stationary boiler whilst '57xx' pannier tank No.3739 waits to be coaled up amidst piles of ash. The coaler looks a little time worn with windows either bricked up or smashed and little in the way of protection from the elements.

Plate 59.  No.40700                25th March 1962                P Askey - Kershaw

Plate 60.  No.53809                26th August 1962                P Askey - Kershaw

It has to be said that today I have a passion for the old Somerset & Dorset and spend much time walking its trackbed, but as a trainspotter back in the 1960s other than the Midland '7F' and '2P' classes I had no interest. Of two visits paid the first was in 1961 on a shed bash with the Home Counties on a 'five minutes lads' basis. No photos but plenty of good cops. Second time with Peter, on 26th August 1962, we stopped off at Bath while going on to Bristol and with no film I thought myself lucky to find a chemist open on a Sunday only to have my hopes dashed because he wouldn't sell me any due the Sunday trading laws.

Plate 61. No.92220 *Evening Star*          26th August 1962          P Askey - Kershaw

Our other problem was catching the next Bristol train, so we had to run to Bath loco sheds there and back. Twenty one locos were on shed with three Midland '7Fs' present including No.53809 (Plate 60) and BR Standard '9F' *Evening Star* itself just prior to working the last 'Pines Express' over the old S&D line. Five months earlier Peter had travelled to Bath and caught LMS '2P' No. 40700 out of steam (Plate 59). She would be the last of the Somerset & Dorset '2P's', being withdrawn in September 1962.

Plates 62. LMS '2Ps' Nos.40563 and 40634          7th September 1961          Kodak 44A

Templecombe was visited in September 1961, courtesy of the Home Counties Railway Club, and by then the piloting exploits of the LMS '2Ps' over the Mendips on the S&D route were no more. They were then relegated to secondary duties and on the day of our visit four were on shed including Nos.40563 and 40634. Of interest No.40634 was one of three purchased by the SDJRly direct from Derby Works on 1928.

Another view of No.2822

Plate 63.  No.2822    6th September 1964    Minolta SR1

Plate 64.  No.6908 *Downham Hall*    6th September 1964    Minolta SR1

Visited on three occasions, the first time in September 1961, which produced some forty four steam and a few diesel shunters, but by my last visit three years later this had collapsed to fifteen steam and eleven diesels. All the photos are from the last visit. One of the last surviving locos of the '28xx' series No.2822 is taking on coal, whilst 'Hall' No.6908 simmers in the yard. The loco shed itself was a single boarded over turntable affair with, by 1964, half the roof missing.

# TAUNTON

Taunton loco shed, September 1961

Plate 65. No.1450    6th September 1964    MinoltaSR1

Plate 66. No.7303                6th September 1964                Minolta SR1

As it was late on in the day, which was now pretty dismal, the lack of roof allowed some photos. By this time Moguls were used on the Barnstaple trains but No.7303 lies out of steam by the stationary boiler which likewise was stone cold, whilst '14xx' tank No.1450 simmers quietly away. This loco, along with one other, was the last to be withdrawn in May 1965. These locos, when in steam, were few and far between and always in awkward positions, so please excuse the camera shake on this picture.

Plate 67. No.4133           23rd September 1962           Fed-2

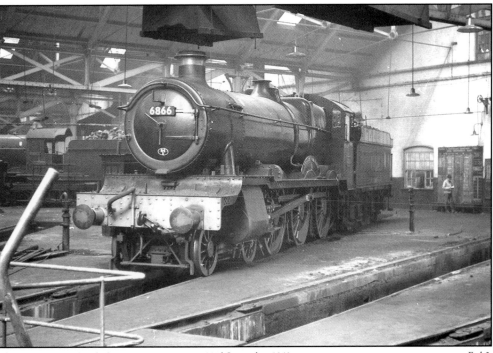

Plate 68. No.6866 *Morfa Grange*       23rd September 1962        Fed-2

The Birmingham area to me means disaster. In retrospect too few trips there, lost films on earlier visits and dreadful weather conditions for the remainder. A day out on 23rd September 1962 rewarded me with a bright interlude at Tyseley but dirty misty rain everywhere else, and on top of that long delays due to diesel failures on the return trip and waiting for a grubby 'Hall' to rescue us from Banbury. Tyseley was similar to Old Oak in construction but held only two turntables of the under-girder type but not boarded over.

Plate 69. No.6971 *Athelhampton Hall*      23rd September 1962      Fed-2

Plate 70. Nos.3660 & 7424      23rd September 1962      Fed-2

Thirty four locos were in steam including, Plates 67 and 68, large Prairie No.4133 and a rather clean 'Grange' No.6866. Note the trainspotter checking his numbers against the duty board. Meanwhile 'Modified Hall' No.6971 simmers outside. Whilst most of the shed's glazing appears to be intact, note the large wooden shed warning sign, then generally ignored, but now a coveted item. Back inside around the turntable are two panniers '74xx' No.7424 and the ubiquitous '57xx' No.3660. By the time Wolverhampton was reached the weather had near closed in.

# GLOUCESTER (HORTON ROAD)

Plate 71.  No.6947 *Helmingham Hall*　　　　22nd September 1963　　　　Mamiya C22

Plate 72.  No.6344　　　　2nd March 1963　　　　Fed-2

A ten road affair whose Great Western influence waned slightly with the closure of Barnwood, the Midland shed, thus showering Horton Road with many LMS locomotives. A rather grimy 'Hall' No.6947 is readying itself for departure whist earlier in the year '43xx' class No.6344 does likewise. Note the wheel drop to the left and one of the gasometers that dominated this part of Gloucester.

# GLOUCESTER (HORTON ROAD)

Plate 73.  No.2241                    2nd March 1963                    Fed-2

Plate 74.  No.73028                    5th July 1964                    Minolta SR1

Two further views show '2251' class No.2241 positioning itself in the shed yard between two water cranes, although one has lost its shute. Standard class '5MT' No.73028 parks up in a quiet corner at the top end of the loco shed yards. On this particular visit there were no less than five '14xx' tanks on shed, none of which availed themselves for photography.

Plate 75. No.5049 *Earl of Devon*        2nd March 1963        Fed-2

Plate 76. No.53807        2nd March 1963        Fed-2

Two strangers on shed. 'Castle' class No.5049 receiving attention to the middle set of driving wheels. Whatever the problem it was insurmountable as she was withdrawn that month. Somerset & Dorset '7F' No.53807 was out of steam, what she was doing here I could not find out but I doubt it has anything to do with the breakdown train. Note the shovel thrown down and the general debris everywhere, this was becoming ever more noticeable by the mid 1960s.

# NEWPORT (EBBW JUNCTION)

Plate 77. Pannier Line up        19th February 1961        Kodak 620 Box Camera

Plate 78. No.2818        2nd March 1963        Fed-2

First time here was in February 1961 and it was apparent this was a freight depot with over one hundred locos on shed. Classes '28xx' and Standard '9Fs' abounded with thirty of the large freight tank engines built for working the South Wales valleys present. English Electric Type 3 diesels were introduced for these workings in late 1962 and within the year they covered all of Ebbw's freight routes and diagrams. By the Summer of 1964 steam could only muster some forty locos with diesels in equal measure.

Plate 79. No.6835 *Eastham Grange*          14th October 1962          Fed-2

Plate 80. No.7244          21st June 1964          Minolta SR1

The general view of Ebbw in Plate 77 shows panniers and tank locos. Up the top end of the yard alongside the coaler ramp is No.2818 having been coaled up (Plate 78) and down by the workshops stands 'Grange' No.6835, not that many named locomotives graced Ebbw (Plate 79). Near the same spot nearly two years later '72xx' large tank No.7244, a rebuild of class '52xx', languishes amongst a line up of English Electric Type 3 diesels.

Plate 81. No.6758 and company      19th February 1961      Kodak 620 Box Camera

Plate 82. No.5244      2nd March 1963      Fed-2

Visited on the same day as Ebbw, Newport Pill sported some thirty four steam locos comprising of all large tanks and panniers, hence the excellent line up alongside the shed with the transporter bridge over the River Usk in the background. Even by this date diesel shunters were present. On a visit in March 1963 steam had collapsed to around thirteen with the depot closing to steam a few months later. Diesel shunters were still in evidence there a year later but apparently the majority were simply left scattered around the docks when not in use.

Plate 83. No.4144                         21st June 1964                         Minolta SR1

Plate 84. No.4248                         2nd March 1963                            Fed-2

Even by 1963 there was still a healthy selection of steam to be seen. Prairie No.4141 positioned in the yard alongside the main running lines which disappointingly, for trainspotters on passing trains, had a large earth bank running alongside the loco yards. Up on the coaler road '42xx' tank No.4248 was one of many waiting to be coaled up, the 'WD' behind was No.90570. I cannot be totally certain but it would appear that a rail mounted crane was assisting coaling up locos or clearing ash.

Plate 85. Nos.9730 & 8701          20th August 1961          Kodak 44A

Plate 86. No.6361          3rd March 1963          Fed-2

An interesting depot being an eight road straight shed built onto an original roundhouse with an allocation of near one hundred locomotives at Nationalisation in 1948. This had dropped by half when I first came here in late 1960. With a staple diet of tank locomotives of all descriptions it could produce some surprises, in March 1963 for example, with nine 'Granges' and six 'Halls'. The top photo shows a general view of the straight shed with some Home Counties club members still milling around.

Plate 87.  No.7251        3rd March 1963        Fed-2

Plate 88.  No.8461        3rd March 1963        Fed-2

On Plate 86 Mogul No.6361 stands at the top end of the yard with the straight shed behind, whilst large tank '72xx' class No.7251 shunts some ash wagons by the water tank at the roundhouse end of the depot on Plate 87. On the coaler road '94xx' No.8461 heads a line up of locomotives in front of what appears to be crane assisted coaling or clearing of ash.

Plate 89. Nos.1611 & 1607      12th July 1964      Minolta SR1

Plate 90. No.7235      12th July 1964      Minolta SR1

Paul and I took a train trip to this lonely outpost of steam on 12th July 1964, my 19th birthday. We were rewarded in passing by train, and then bunking in, R S Hayes nearby scrap yard. All other local steam depots had gone by this time so we did Newport Ebbw on the way back. I suppose looking tired and weary an old couple gave us a few pennies to catch the bus back to the station. Still forty two steam locos presented themselves at Llanelly including five '16xx' tanks, two in the top photo, while the other photo represents the victors and the vanquished.

Plate 91.  No.7900 *Saint Peters Hall*                    21st June 1964                    Minolta SR1

Plate 92.  No.6656                    14th October 1962                    Fed-2

This depot was a mystery to me for during the early 1960s I thought it closed in 1958 and only saw reference to it in photographs of long gone Welsh tank locos. Latter day reading indicates it was a depot for Cardiff docks diesel shunters. However following a visit to Cardiff in October 1962 and a three o'clock in the morning visit to a part demolished Canton depot it appeared that Cardiff East Dock was back in business.

Plate 93. No.5951 *Clyffe Hall*                    14th October 1962                    Fed-2

Plate 94. No.6845 *Paviland Grange*               14th October 1962                    Fed-2

East Dock was a 'Loan Act' shed, built in 1931, similar to Didcot in construction but of eight roads. Plate 91 shows 'Modified Hall' No.7900 outside the shed. In Plate 92 '56xx' No.6656 takes on coal from a coaling plant never exactly designed for large tender engines which were now a common feature here. Another little problem at East Dock was the lack of a turntable as it had been a tanky shed all its life until the Cardiff area's 'Indian Summer' of steam.

Plate 95. No.6931 *Aldborough Hall*          14th October 1962                              Fed-2

Plate 96. No.92219                        21st June 1964                              Minolta SR1

On our initial 1962 visit to East Dock which always involved a degree of 'daring do' to avoid the police on dock entrances, Canton's overflow made East Dock a very busy place with seventy locos on including nine 'Castles' and twenty two 'Halls' and 'Granges'. By the Summer of 1964 this had dropped back to around thirty, the depot finally closing one year later. Of interest during its earlier 'closure', BR sold the land and then had to rent it back for its reincarnation.

# BARRY

Plate 97.  Nos.5657 & 5688                      21st June 1964                      Minolta SR1

Plate 98.  No.5669                              21st June 1964                      Minola SR1

Better known for its dump. The shed was a good solid brick built six road depot with a north light pattern roof opened in 1897. Barry was always a tank shed and in all my visits I only ever saw three tender locos, a 'Grange' and a Midland 'Black 5' and an '8F', all on the same occasion in June 1964. Barry closed to steam three months later and on, what was to be the first pilgrimage to Barry dump in January 1965, a quick visit to the depot revealed ten diesels.

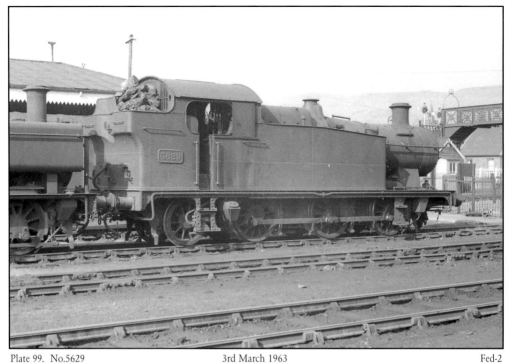

Plate 99.  No.5629                  3rd March 1963                  Fed-2

Plate 100.  No.6670                  3rd March 1963                  Fed-2

Two small South Wales loco depots. Abercynon was a Government 'Loan Act ' shed built in 1929 whilst Llantrisant was a stone built affair dating from 1900. Both visited on a two day coach trip courtesy of the Home Counties Railway Club. The photographs are unusual in that the sun was shining, not a common occurrence in my experience whilst travelling up, down and around the South Wales Valleys.

Plate 101. No.5237          3rd March 1963          Fed-2

Plate 102. No.3717          3rd March 1963          Fed-2

A standard GW single roundhouse depot built in 1907. By the early sixties around forty locos could be guaranteed on shed with the normal South Wales diet of '42xx', '56xx' and panniers tanks plus a few tender engines. As this visit was on the same day as the preceding page the sun was out dispelling the gloom and so allowed a few indoor photographs to be taken. Club trips would mean no time for erecting tri-pods so it was a case of camera settings to maximum aperture and 1/30th sec exposure to avoid camera shake.

# CAERPHILLY WORKS

Plate 103. Caerphilly Works        19th February 1961        Kodak 620 Box Camera

Plate 104. No.4650        14th October 1962        Fed-2

Built by the Rhymney Railway in 1900 for locomotive repairs only, no locomotives having been built here. A few visits were made from 1961 onwards and in that time the locos 'on works' for repair dropped dramatically. Locomotives were certainly cut up here and during February 1961 Nos.1143 (see Plate 341), 6411 and 9737 were being dealt with, and on my last visit in March 1963 Nos. 4266 and 6672 were undergoing the same fate. A general view can be seen in the top photo.

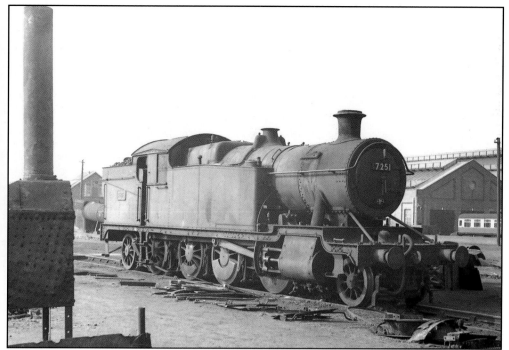

Plate 105.  No.7251                    14th October 1962                    Fed-2

Plate 106.  NCB former GW No.443       14th October 1962                    Fed-2

The remaining photos date from October 1962 showing pannier tank No.4650 (Plate 104) under repair and large tank No.7251 outside and, interestingly, inside the old carriage paint shop was a former Taff Vale class 'O1' tank. This became GW No.450 and was sold off initially to the army and then onto a colliery 'up North', the NCB finally presenting it for preservation. Dieselisation and the new repair centre at Cardiff Canton finished Caerphilly off in June 1963, No.450 being the last loco to leave the works.

Plate 107.  No.5070 *Sir Daniel Gooch*          25th November 1962                                    Fed-2

Plate 108.  No.5322                              25th November 1962                                    Fed-2

Shrewsbury was a 'one off' train trip for me, notable that, yet again, I suffered another 'Western' diesel failure. The shed was a large complex with an LMS long shed built alongside a Great Western roundhouse. 'Castle' No.5070 is seen by the coaler on the GW side which by this time was, as I recall, out of use with the roundhouse derelict. Mogul No.5322 is on the LMS side and with sixty three active steam 'on shed' including twenty two Midland jobbies, it was only a few months before the depot was transferred to the Midland region.

Plate 109. No.7800 *Torquay Manor*        23rd December 1962        Fed-2

Plate 110. No.1666        23rd December 1962        Fed-2

Last trip of 1962 was to Oswestry and Croes Newydd with no permits. Oswestry was a six road straight shed and certainly worth the visit with twenty five 'on' including '14xx' ,'16xx' , five 'Manors' and no less than nine Ivatt '2MT' tender locos on shed. Of four dumped behind the shed, pannier tank No.7428 which was withdrawn two months previous still proudly retained, for all the world to see, G.W.R on her pannier sides. Of the photos taken at Croes Newydd there is no trace.

## NINE ELMS

Plate 111.  Front Ends          5th April 1964          Mamiya C22

Plate 112.  No.30039          13th January 1963          Fed-2

A large twenty five road dead end straight depot built in two stages. The original part became known as the 'Old Shed' whilst the latter the 'New Shed'. To hop off a No.77 bus from Clapham at the Brooklands Road bus stop and look down this gently descending cul-de-sac of drab Victorian terrace housing and bomb sites, Nine Elms Motive Power Depot was there for all to see. A panoramic view of noise and movement, whistles and steam as locomotives came and went to the fantastic backdrop of Battersea Power Station.

Plate 113. Nos.30586/87     25th May 1963     Mamiya C22

Plate 114. No.30921     25th May 1963     Mamiya C22

This part of London and Nine Elms itself had suffered heavy bombing during the war and much of the housing around the loco yards had been replaced with new flats. Some twenty years on half of the 'Old Shed' was still without a roof and had no smoke troughs whatsoever, giving more of an appearance of a giant barn than a loco depot. Plate 111 shows a line up of BR Standards parked up outside the truncated 'Old Shed' with the 'New Shed' behind. Just three years earlier this would have produced a very different brood of engines.

Plate 115. No.30839          25th May 1963          Mamiya C22

Plate 116. No.31627          7th July 1963          Mamiya C22

'M7', 'E4X' tanks and GW panniers were regular performers on ECS duties out of Waterloo station. These classes declined as BR Standard class '3MT' tanks (Plate 124) were introduced from late 1962 onwards. 'M7' No.30039 (Plate 112) was still usefully employed until withdrawn in February 1963, the last of the Nine Elms' allocated 'M7s'. Several 'M7s' were reported working at Nine Elms following withdrawal, No.30032 on ECS in June 1963 and Nos.30249 and 30111 on loco shed shunting duties as late as September 1963 and February 1964.

Plate 117.  No.31924                    5th April 1964                    Mamiya C22

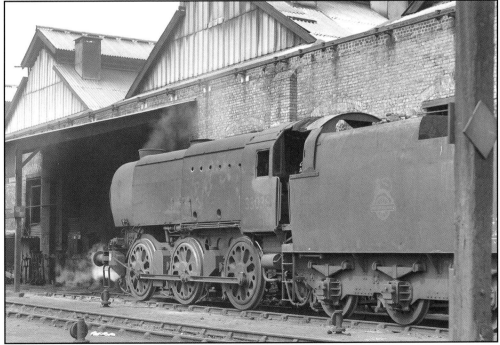

Plate 118.  No.33039                    7th July 1963                    Mamiya C22

Visitors to Nine Elms were all three surviving class '0298' well tanks when they came up to London from Eastleigh to work a SLS 'South Western Suburban Special' on 2nd December 1962. Plate 113 shows Nos.30586/87 with No.30585 out of view stored in the 'New Shed' which, with a complete roof and smoke troughs, could be rather gloomy. All were withdrawn in December and one at least was still present in October 1963.

Plate. 119.  No.34070 *Manston*          27th July 1963          Mamiya C22

Plate 120.  No.34109 *Sir Trafford Leigh- Mallory*     9th August 1964     Minolta SR1

Failing to retain any photographs of 'Schools' on Nine Elms prior to their final demise in December 1962, Plate 114 shows No.30921 stored in the 'Old Shed'. With weeks to go prior to withdrawal Nine Elms' last few 'Schools' including No.30921 were noted running nameless out of Waterloo on parcel trains. The 'S15s' were never allocated to Nine Elms and Plate 115 shows No.30839 pulling off shed, possibly booked on a Basingstoke or Salisbury service which they frequently worked during the summer of '63.

Plate 121. No.35014 *Nederland Line*          9th August 1964          Minolta SR1

Plate 122. No.35016 *Elders Fyffes*          13th October 1963          Mamiya C22

Nine Elms always had a small allocation of SR Moguls for local freight workings, but within a year of No.31627 (Plate 116) coming off the turntable, Nine Elms allocation had all been withdrawn. The 'W' tanks were elusive on Nine Elms and No.31924 (Plate 117) was working out her remaining months on ECS duties. Note the original remaining 'Old Shed' pillars none of which were ever removed after the war. 'Q1' No.33039 (Plate 118) was an Eastleigh loco, the remainder of the class were allocated to Nine Elms from July 1965 onwards.

Plate 123.  No.80143                    7th July 1963                    Mamiya C22

Plate 124.  No.82016                    9th August 1964                    Minolta SR1

Nine Elms meant express passenger duties and Plate 120 shows a rebuilt 'Battle of Britain' No.34109 outside the 'New Shed' alongside the impressive mechanical coaler whilst 'Merchant Navy' No.35014 (Plate 121) stands alongside a derelict crane, taking on water prior to moving onto the turntable. Note, due to the war, the differing house styles at this period. BR Standard '4MT' tanks were relatively unknown at Nine Elms until officially allocated here from November 1964 onwards, of which No.80143 is an example.

# FELTHAM

Plate 125.  No.30035
5th August 1962
Fed-2

Plate 126.  No.30346
3rd February 1962
P.Askey - Minolta A5

Feltham was approached down along a long cinder path through allotments and always seemed to be, on a Sunday, a quiet countryside loco shed. A seemingly modern depot of concrete construction despite being built in the 1920s it could house some real relics including classes '0395' and '700' light freight locos and 'O2' and 'M7' tanks, and could sport the occasional 'King Arthur'.

Plate 127. No.30494                    5th August 1962                    P.Askey - Kershaw

Plate 128. No.30520                    5th August 1962                    Kodak Retinette 1A

Two locomotive classes forever associated with Feltham were the 'G16' and 'H16' tank engines for working the extensive marshalling yards there. The top picture shows 'G16' No.30494 in store in August 1962, the class being withdrawn by December. Whereas in the lower picture 'H16' No.30520 is steaming onto shed in the Summer of 1962, however the whole class was withdrawn by November but one, No.30517, was reported working until Christmas Eve 1962.

# FELTHAM

Plate 129.  No.30512                    15th September 1963                    Mamiya C22

Plate 130.  No.30840                    29th March 1964                    Mamiya C22

Of the 'S15' mixed traffic locos Feltham was home to the complete batch of the original LSWRly Urie version and the vast majority of the latter day Southern Maunsell types. The top picture shows Urie version No.30512 with original eight wheel tender, this loco was to be the last of the class being withdrawn in March 1964. The lower picture depicts the Maunsell version with modified eight wheel tender. The last few survivors were withdrawn from Feltham in September 1965.

Plate 131. No.33027          15th November 1964          Minolta SR1

Plate 132. No.33038          7th August 1963          Mamiya C22

Another class which was always associated with Feltham was the Austerity build 'Q1' freight locos of the war period. Although hideous in appearance they were reputedly excellent machines and well over half the class were allocated to Feltham over the years. No.33027 was photographed in November 1964 when Feltham's last remaining 'Q1s' were transferred to Nine Elms. Sister loco No.33038 is outside the single road repair shop, the height of the building reflecting a fifty ton overhead crane being installed there.

Plate 133.  No.73170　　　　　　8th March 1964　　　　　　Mamiya C22

Plate 134  No.75066　　　　　　15th November 1964　　　　　　Minolta SR1

Of the BR Standard types, the class '5's were transferred in from September 1963 but the class '4' 4-6-0s never were allocated to Feltham. No 75066 was a visitor from Eastleigh. From June 1963 onwards class '4' tanks and '9Fs' were allocated. On one occasion we were purloined by the foreman who pointing to the steam engines inferred we ought to photograph them all before being replaced by diesels. Sadly I doubt that he realised, nor us, that not only would steam go but also the motive power depot, the marshalling yards, and everything else.

# GUILDFORD & WINCHESTER

Plate 135.  No.30089                    26th February 1962                    Kodak Retinette 1A

Plate 136.  No.30096                    11th February 1962                    Kodak Retinette 1A

These two depots had the last class 'B4' duties. No.30089 was the Guildford shed pilot until replaced by a 'USA' tank in March 1963 which left classmate No.30096 working the Winchester station yard from its corrugated iron shed until October 1963. On being retired both were withdrawn, No.30096 being the last of the class to go. Unlike the train trip to Winchester and Eastleigh on a bright Winter's day Guildford, two weeks earlier, was a misery driving down the old A3 on a Raleigh moped in driving snow. Not recommended.

Plate 137. No.30903 *Charterhouse*          30th September 1962          Fed-2

Plate 138. No.31819          14th July 1963          Mamiya C22

Reading South, despite being a sub shed to Guildford, was always a active little depot. Passenger duties included the Reading to Redhill service which meant initially 'Schools' and Southern Mogul classes would always be found on shed. The depot officially closed with the end of steam on this service from 1st January 1965. However it must have largely gone out of use by the Summer of 1964 because Southern engines from then on were comparatively common in the GW shed.

# READING SOUTH

Plate 139.  No.31620       23rd February 1964       Mamiya C22

Plate 140.  No.31625       30th September 1962       Fed-2

The 'Schools' class were active on the Reading to Redhill diagram until withdrawal in December 1962 and Plate 137 shows No.30903 on the buffers at the rear of the shed. The Southern Moguls held sway but by late 1964 these had mostly given way to BR Standard class '4' tanks. Plate 138 is interesting as it shows the front of the depot with a new age dawning, a high rise office block under construction. Eventually redevelopment of this area was something which would sweep away all evidence of Southern railway facilities.

Plate 141. No.30765 *Sir Gareth*          25th March 1962          Kodak Retinette 1A

Plate 142. No.30934 *St Lawrence*          25th March 1962          Kodak Retinette 1A

My first visit here was in March 1962 following on from a train trip to Eastleigh catching a semi fast back up to Basingstoke hauled by a 'Lord Nelson'. With 'King Arthurs' and 'Schools' classes in steam on shed this was the last time which I would really see the old order. No.30765, which along with No.30770, were Basingstoke engines and the last 'King Arthurs' on the books. Likewise 'Schools' class No.30934 survived until the end of 1962, both classes here remaining active on London semi fasts, secondary duties and parcel trains up to the end.

Plate 143.  No.33009                    26th July 1964                    Minolta SR1

Plate 144.  No.34022 *Exmoor*            18th August 1963                    Mamiya C22

On following visits up to 1964 diesels never played much part at Basingstoke and although never more than twenty locos would be present a good mix of freight and Pacifics could always be seen. 'Q1' No.33009 is seen outside the three road depot whilst the lower picture evokes a period before health and safety with the young fireman taking a ride on the buffer beam of No.34022 running on to the depot following switching points.

# FRATTON

No.32678 February 1962

Plate 145.  Fratton Loco Shed and yards          26th July 1964          P.Askey - Minolta A5

Plate 146.  No.32650          14th April 1963          Mamiya C22

Closed in 1959 Fratton remained an active depot and the Hayling Island 'A1X' Terrier tanks were located here. From around 1962 onwards it became a holding place for locomotives awaiting possible preservation including Nos.30120, 30245, 30587, 30777, 30850, 30925, 30926, 30950, 30951, 31725 and 31757 being stored there at various times until September 1964 when the last examples were moved to Stratford Works.

Plate 147.  Fratton Loco Shed                    14th April 1963                    P.Askey - Minolta A5

Plate 148.  No.30062                    29th October 1961                    P.Askey - Kershaw

A selection of stored locos are viewed in Plate147. The depot suffered heavy bomb damage during the war and this may be a result in the total lack of smoke troughs. Following on from a visit to Eastleigh in October 1961 we managed to gain entry into Southampton Docks with 'USA' tanks still active, working over some eighty miles of docklands trackwork. Eight months later the first diesels appeared and by November 1962 steam had gone.

Plate 149. Nos. 20 & 21        7th August 1963        P.Askey - Minolta A5

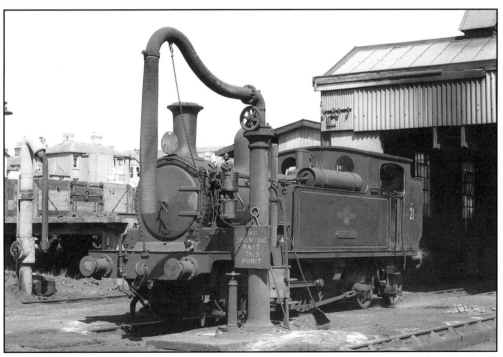

Plate 150. No.21        7th August 1963        P.Askey - Minolta A5

Peter Askey and Paul Wells weekend trip to the Isle of Wight which sadly I could not go on due to work. On their return I was not impressed with sleeping on a park bench but in recent years I wish I had joined them. The top picture shows a general view of the depot with the coal stage sporting a canopy which gives a quaint railway station appearance. Steam lasted on the island until 1967 being replaced by old electric London Underground stock with which I was very familiar.

Plate 151.  No.75072                    27th September 1964                    Minolta SR1

Plate 152.  No.92206                    29th September 1963                    Mamiya C22

A large fifteen road straight through depot with little in the way of atmosphere. With a roof covering five pitches at the end of each roof pitch corrugated steel sheeting had been put up in BR days with large painted black squares. Absolutely no idea why but makes for easy identification in photographs. In spite of being an 'A' shed, on a Sunday there was little going on and whilst the North 'front' end was generally devoid of activity the back could see rows and rows of dead engines. Never, ever, a problem walking round this sprawling complex.

Plate 153. Nos.34027 *Taw Valley* & 30850 *Lord Nelson* 11th February 1962        Kodak Retinette 1A

Plate 154. No.30530        25th August 1963        Mamiya C22

Showing the black squares off to maximum effect at the North end of the depot. Plate 151 shows No.75072 with, as a backdrop, part of the large water tank. '9F' No 92206, Plate 152, a double chimney version, was a regular performer on the Fawley petrol block trains. Meanwhile a bit of action in Plate 153 when 'Lord Nelson' class No.30850 blows off steam prior to moving out as 'West Country' No.34027 backs in.

Plate 155.  No.34007 *Wadebridge*          18th August 1963          Mamiya C22

Plate 156.  No.76013          26th July 1964          Minolta SR1

Eastleigh had a large six tip coaler served by a wagon ramp more common to the Great Western Railway. This was supplemented from about 1964 by a mobile steam crane and grab. Plates 154, 155 and 156 illustrate various locomotives being coaled up. Large Southern depots generally had mechanical coalers, for example Nine Elms, and although one was planned for Eastleigh in the 1930s it never materialised.

Plate 157. No.34061 *73 Squadron*          26th July 1964          P.Askey - Minolta A5

No.32636     March 1964

Plate 158. No.34079     7th February 1965     Minolta SR1

By the early 1960s once inside this sprawling depot it always seemed half empty. Roofing repairs after the war may explain the lack of smoke troughs and this gave the effect of being literally 'in a shed'. With the majority of locomotives being out of steam Eastleigh never had that sometimes claustrophobic feel of busy loco shed. However the photographs above did reassure you you were on the Southern, and even that started to change.

Plate 159.  No.30133       22nd March 1964       Mamiya C22

Plate 160.  No.30667       26th July 1964       Minolta SR1

Class 'M7' tanks had always been a part of Eastleigh and both pictures above depict the class at the end of their working life. Doing a bit of shunting alongside the water tank No.30133 was withdrawn by the end of the month whilst push and pull version shows No.30667 which actually started life as No.30106. Early in 1961 this loco came out of works as No.30667. Now just withdrawn this photograph shows off the back of the depot and yard to some effect, although somewhat empty even for 1964.

Plate 161. No.30773 *Sir Lavaine*          25th March 1962          Kodak Retinette 1A

Plate 162. No.30857 *Lord Howe*          11th February 1962          Kodak Retinette 1A

Many locos would be lined up in the yards at the rear of Eastleigh depot and two class stalwarts of Eastleigh were the 'Lord Nelsons' and the 'King Arthurs'. Although Basingstoke was the last home for the few remaining 'Arthurs', No.30773 was one of the last remaining of Eastleigh's own. The 'Nelsons' had all been allocated to Eastleigh for years and alongside the newly built diesel depot No.30857 is, on this visit, one of six remaining. At this late stage they could still be seen on Southampton boat trains as well as local and parcel turns.

Plate 163.  No.31723         11th February 1962         Kodak Retinette 1A

Plate 164.  No.31890         25th August 1963         Mamiya C22

With motion part obscured by heaps of ash class 'C' No.31723 is dwafed between a 'Lord Nelson' and some BR Standard classes. She was a Guildford loco, now out of steam, and facing withdrawal. Another interesting class were the 'U1' Moguls and the bulk of them had been withdrawn at the end of 1962. Four struggled on into 1963 and No.31890 was one of these. Interestingly she was a solitary rebuild of the 'K1' 'River' class 2-6-4 tank loco.

Plate 165. No.31925                    10th November 1963                    Mamiya C22

Plate 166. No.35025 *Brocklebank Line*         18th August 1963                    Mamiya C22

Class 'W' tanks spent their working lives on freights around the London area but a few were transferred in late 1962 to Exmouth Junction for banking duties. No.31925 is a former Norwood engine. The old coaler plant is to the right of the picture with cranes having been drafted in for coaling or clearing ash. Meanwhile 'Merchant Navy' class No.35025 was one of the original 1956 rebuilds and was withdrawn one year following on from this photograph.

Plate 167.  Main  Repair Shops     14th April 1963     P.Askey - Minolta A5

Plate 168.  No.34078 *222 Squadron*     14th April 1963     Mamiya C22

Eastleigh Loco Shed may have been a pushover but the Works was another proposition. Permits were the order of the day and the few 'unofficial' visits always landed up in heavy handed exit. One occasion Peter Askey and myself were frogmarched from the Works to the Gatehouse to, we were impolitely informed, have the book thrown at us. Sadly we were confronted by 'The Authority' doing his knitting. Now a man can't do what a man's got to do whilst knitting. Even as he ranted and raved the tears of laughter started running down our cheeks.

Plate 169.  No.30120                         29th October 1961                                   Kodak 44A

Plate 170.  No.30850 *Lord Nelson*           25th March 1962                          Kodak Retinette 1A

A Works visit, with a Permit, on the 14th April 1963, Plates 167 and 168, produced thirty six steam locomotives the majority being Southern Moguls and light Pacifics. By the end of 1961 one 'T9' remained No.30120 which was dumped in a siding outside the Works whilst the last one to be scrapped, No.30287, had just been cut up. Some six months later around the back, tucked away by itself in a corner, lies No.30850 *Lord Nelson*. Both locomotives were not withdrawn at the time of the photographs but I doubt they ever turned another wheel until after preservation.

Plate 171. No.34001 *Exeter*        24th September 1961        Kodak 44A

Plate 172. Nos.34104 *Bere Alston* & 31801      25th July 1963      P.Askey - Minolta A5

If Eastleigh was quiet then Bournemouth most certainly was not. These pictures show the depot for what it was, all Pacifics and a good smattering of 'M7' tanks which worked the branch lines in the area, the last one going in May 1964. Southern Moguls were never allocated to Bournemouth in any numbers and on our visits were few and far between, and class 'U' No.31801, an Eastleigh engine, looks to be in for some running repairs.

Plate 173. No.30056                    2nd August 1963                    Mamiya C22

Plate 174. Nos.30530 & 35015 *Rotterdam Lloyd*    24th September 1961                    Kodak 44A

Bournemouth was set on a crowded site tucked in between the main running lines and suburbia and if memory serves me right there were large signs exulting enginemen to keep noise to a minimum. For unofficial entry, and otherwise, one could slip in through the rear but for some reason there were no steps down but a steep ramp which was unusual. Years later, when the yard had become a car park and the shed walls had been cut right down, the ramp remained . . . going to nowhere.

# BOURNEMOUTH

Plate 175.  No.75065                    17th May 1964                    Minolta SR1

Plate 176.  Nos.82027/28                17th May 1964                    Minolta SR1

Standard classes had made little impact at Bournemouth until the class '4' 2-6-0s arrived in numbers during the early 1960s. BR Standard class '4' 4-6-0 No.75065 photographed here alongside the depot's electric crane was one of a few allocated to Bournemouth for a short time. BR Standard tanks became common from the mid 1960s and a few class '3' 2-6-2Ts stayed for a short time. The larger class '4' variety worked here in some numbers to the end of steam.

GW types, September 1961

Plate 177. No.34070 *Manston*     17th May 1964     Minolta SR1

Plate 178. No.34088 *213 Squadron*     17th May 1964     P.Wells - Kodak 44A

I only went to Weymouth twice with near three years apart, initially in September 1961 and then again in May 1964, and on both occasions twenty four steam were present. However in the intervening years the depot had seen a total turnabout. Transferring to the Southern Region in 1958 Great Western types still dominated in 1961 with only a handful of Southern present. By 1964 a single GW loco remained with nine Southern types mainly light Pacifics, four Midland Ivatt tanks and the remainder BR Standard tender classes.

Plate 179. Nos.73018 & 34071 *601 Squadron*  17th May 1964  Minolta SR1

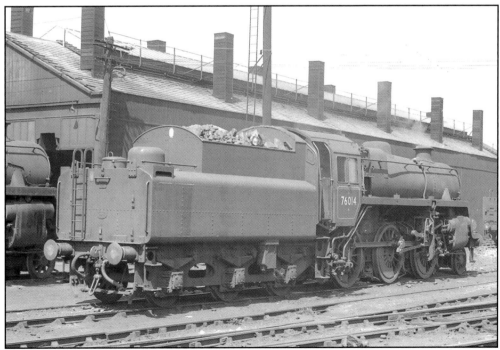

Plate 180. No.76014  17th May 1964  Minolta SR1

All the photographs are from May 1964 and Plates 177 and 178 are of 'Battle of Britain' class light Pacifics, both getting ready for the road. No.34070 steams past the coaler whilst No.34088 has just turned ready for coaling up. Both these locos have a bit of history, No.34070 pulled the last scheduled steam hauled Plymouth train out of Brighton in January 1964. Although allocated to Nine Elms No.34088 was 'loaned' to Stewarts Lane during 1963 for Royal train workings as this depot was known for its high standards of engine preparation.

Plate 181. No.30670                    17th September 1961                    Kodak 44A

Plate 182. No.30953                    17th September 1961                    Kodak 44A

Exmouth Junction depot was reached following a long drawn out Home Counties Railway Club coach trip to the West Country in September 1961. Sadly I missed the class '700' and 'T9's these had gone by the Summer but the 'M7' and the 'Z' tanks remained, caught by my plastic camera on a none too bright a day . . . and none too bright a picture. The 'M7' tanks worked the Exmouth branch until April 1963 and that was the end of them, whilst the 'Z' class had gone wholesale at the end of 1962.

Plate 183.  No.31843                          23rd February 1964                          Mamiya C22

Plate 184.  No.34013 *Okehampton*          6th September 1964                          Minolta SR1

In January 1963 west of Salisbury came under the control of the Western Region and by September 1964 the former Southern main line was being downgraded with the 'Atlantic Coast Express' already a casualty. With less than a year to go until closure, diesels and pannier tanks had made their presence felt and steam numbers were already in decline. Western pannier tanks had replaced the large 'W' tanks which had been bought down from London to replace the original 'Z' tanks for banking duties.

Plate 185. No.34061 *73 Squadron*         23rd February 1964         Mamiya C22

Plate 186. No.35026 *Lamport & Holt Line*      23rd February 1964        Mamiya C22

Southern Pacifics had always been associated with Exmouth Junction but with main line steam in rapid decline some of the first rebuilds were withdrawn from here in June 1964. Likewise Southern Moguls were always well represented on shed (Plate 183) but by late 1964 all were stored out of use in the shed yard whilst many Pacifics were lined up in sidings opposite the running depot. Always of interest are engine crew and the driver of No.34061 seems to be sizing me up - 'bloody trainspotters'.

Ivatt tank No.41284, September 1964

Plate 187.  No.73161          6th September 1964          Minolta SR1

Plate 188.  No.80039                    6th September 1964                    Minolta SR1

Other than the lightweight class '3' 2-6-2 tanks the British Railways Standard classes had never troubled Exmouth Junction. By the Summer of 1962 a dozen the larger class '4' 2-6-4 tanks were allocated with No.80039 alongside the depot coupled up to an Ivatt tank. Of the LMS Ivatt tanks, note insert, nearly thirty were allocated over the years and several were present on closure in June 1965. A handful of class '5' 4-6-0s were transferred in from September 1963, No.73161 above was the first to be allocated.

Plate 189.  Nos.31842 & 30798 *Sir Hectimere*        24th September 1961                          Kodak 44A

Exeter (St Davids) depot, September 1961.

Plate 190.  Exeter Loco yards                    6th September 1964                          Minolta SR1

Yeovil always had a mixed allocation of Southern and Western engines and this was reflected in my only visit in 1961. Southern locos boasted a good variety including a 'King Arthur' No.30798, the Western could only manage tank engines. Whilst the Southern types had gone by 1964 the panniers lasted until the depot's closure in 1965. Strictly speaking not a Southern depot, Exeter (St Davids) had by 1963 closed to steam. The depot still remained active for diesel stabling purposes but withdrawn Southern locos had migrated down the hill from Exmouth Junction awaiting the scrap man.

Plate 191. No.75067          27th July 1963          Mamiya C22

Plate 192. Stewarts Lane Loco shed        25th May 1963        Mamiya C22

Photographed in 1963 the huge bonded warehouse then seemingly owned by Decca overshadowed the loco shed and yard. By this time Stewarts Lane loco shed was near to closure and is viewed from the footbridge which threaded its way from a short cul-de-sac over electrified tracks and literally through a giant railway viaduct arch. In the late 1950s etc Stewarts Lane, unlike Nine Elms, was heard but not seen, mostly hidden away from gazing eyes by high walls, industrial buildings and old terraced housing. Note minor alterations for diesel traction on the right of the lower picture.

Plate 193. No.75075       27th July 1963       Mamiya C22

Plate 194. No.30928 *Stowe*       25th May 1963       Mamiya C22

Just about able to bunk in a few times from 1960 I managed to get some flavour of the place. The huge dusty coaler standing higher than the railway viaduct whose arches crossed the locomotive yards and running depot itself, the whole scene dominated by the Victorian warehouse, a backdrop to many photographs over many years. Sadly 'Schools' class No.30928 is now withdrawn but classes 'C' and 'N' Nos.31510 (Plate 195) and 31823 (Plate 196) have a few months each to go. The mechanical coaler was the last built by the Southern and it was demolished in 1961 two years before closure.

Plate 195. No.31510        18th February 1962        Kodak Retinette 1A

Plate 196. No.31823        7th July 1963        Mamiya C22

British Railways Standard class '4' No.75075 (Plate 193) was one of the few Standard types allocated here. Of interest is the asbestos 'traverse northlight' roof, one of the improvements made by the Southern Railway during the 1930s. More famous for its two 'Britannias', allocated here in 1958, and class '5' 4-6-0s which all went by the end of the 1950s, a few class '4' 4-6-0s and 2-6-4Ts, see Plate 200, were allocated here from the early 1960s until closure.

Plate 197. No.31305           7th July 1963           Mamiya C22

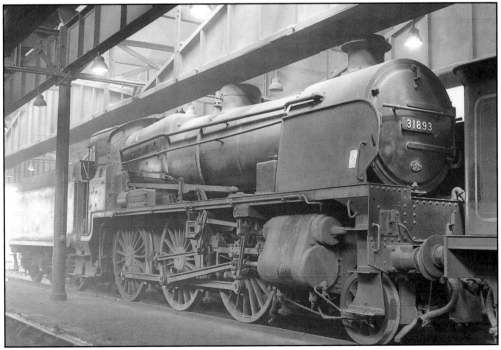

Plate 198. No.31893           7th July 1963           Mamiya C22

By 1963 the depot had transferred from the Eastern to the Central Division of the Southern Region. The number of active steam locomotives then greatly diminished and Stewarts Lane became a collecting point for stored locomotives. One of Stewart Lane's last class 'H' tanks No.31305, now stored, finished its working life during November 1962 on the Kensington Olympia to Clapham Junction service. Likewise three cylinder Mogul 'U1' No.31893 is stored following withdrawal and was one of the last cut up in May 1964.

Plate 199. No.32340          25th May 1963          Mamiya C22

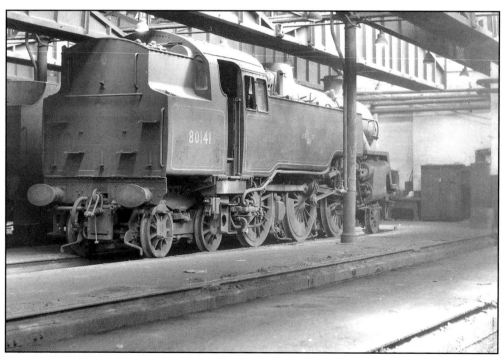

Plate 200. No.80141          27th July 1963          Mamiya C22

LBSC engines were always allocated to Stewarts Lane and class 'C2X' and 'E2' tanks were still to be seen up to 1961 but the 'K' class Moguls did not arrive in numbers until put in store. The top picture shows No.32340 shortly after arrival. This depot more than any other caused me grief but of many memories is Buster and I watching one of 'The Lanes' 'Britannias' in full 'Golden Arrow' regalia coming onto shed alongside the old iron fencing of Stewarts Road and being given a penny each by a old drunk as he stumbled out of a corner pub.

Plate 201.  No.32343                    18th February 1962                    Kodak Retinette 1A

Plate 202.  Nos.32343 & 31719            18th February 1962                    Kodak Retinette 1A

Both photographs were taken on a damp misty day in February 1962, four months before closure. The view from Dunton Road bridge shows the coaling plant and part of the extensive goods yards. Only twenty one steam locos were on shed compared with double that a year previous. Generally visited at dusk, to us young suburban lads 'The Brick' and the surrounding area always presented a brooding atmosphere. A rambling loco shed partially bombed out, as was the area, it was at times nigh on impossible to get into, not helped by once finding ourselves on the roof of the railway police.

Plate 203.  No.31308                    7th January 1962                    Kodak Retinette 1A

Plate 204.  No.31065                    7th January 1962                    Kodak Retinette 1A

Following the Kent Coast electrification project, steam was just about up by the time of our visit here in early 1962. Diesels outnumbered the steam by two to one and a handful of class '24s', transferred from the Midland Region to the Southern in 1959, were still present. An example can be seen behind 'H' tank No.31308. Last remaining 'O1' No.31065 is stored out of use in front of an old steam crane. The loco was later moved to the works where by 1965 she remained with motion removed waiting scrap haulage (it never happened!).

Plate 205.  No.30924 *Haileybury*          7th January 1962          Kodak Retinette 1A

Plate 206.  No.30920 *Rugby*          7th January 1962          Kodal Retinette 1A

A class long associated with the Kent Coast was the 'Schools' and two examples remained on our visit. On the depot was No.30924 a former Bricklayers Arms engine being transferred to Redhill in August 1961 and would be withdrawn the month of the photograph. No.30920 was a former Brighton loco withdrawn the previous month. Situated in the works yard less nameplates, both locomotives would shortly be cut up, a fate shared by many Eastern Section engines, many actually working their one way tickets to Ashford.

# TONBRIDGE

Plate 207.  No.31518          31st December 1961          Kodak Retinette 1A

Plate 208.  No.31639          2nd August 1964          Minolta SR1

A trip here on New Year's Eve 1961 from London by Greenline bus found me getting home in 1962 thanks to heavy snow falling all day. Yes, even then, everything ground to a halt. 'H' tank No.31518 was one of twenty locos on shed, but six months later Tonbridge had lost its own allocation. Amazingly two years on Tonbridge had become a pocket of steam and, despite the influx of diesels, steam did not finish here until 1965.

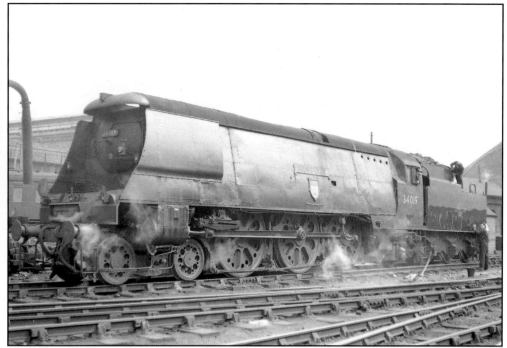

Plate 209. No.34019 *Bideford*          18th April 1963          P.Askey - Minolta A5

Plate 210. No.80068          18th April 1963          P.Askey - Minolta A5

Old photographs of Brighton show a depot with distinctive white edged arched entrances and tiled roof. Whilst the large water tank retained the original Brighton look the loco shed gained an asbestos Northlight pattern roof just prior to the Second World War. Brighton's light Pacifics, of which No.34019 was one, were finished by the end of the 1963 Summer season, however appearances on Plymouth trains continued until January 1964.

Plate 211. No.30543                    10th February 1963                              Fed-2

Plate 212. No.31543                    18th April 1963                        P.Askey - Minolta A5

'Q' class No.30543 is run up against the snowplough in part of the depot which was never re-roofed following the Southern modifications in the late 1930s, She stayed until the depot's closure in June 1964 and finished her days at Redhill being the last to go. The 'H' tanks came to Brighton in the Summer of 1959 as a result of electrification of the Eastern section replacing many 'M7' tanks, however all had been transferred away by 1961. No.31543 has wandered down from Tunbridge Wells West and within three months would be withdrawn.

Plate 213.  No.32417                    22nd April 1962                    Kodak Retinette 1A

Plate 214.  No.32468                    10th February 1963                    Fed-2

Of the old large 'Brighton' tanks all had gone by the end of 1963. The 'Lancing Belle', a workman's train from Brighton to Lancing carriage works was regularly hauled by class 'E6' tanks and the top picture shows No.32417 one of two here which lasted until the end of 1962. Class 'E4' No.32468 was withdrawn in January 1963 after crashing into the buffers whilst working the Kemp Town goods, sister engine No.32479 being the last to go in June 1963 having been displaced by diesels from working the Newhaven Docks duty.

Plate 215. No.30901 *Winchester*     7th September 1962     P.Wells - Kodak 44A

Plate 216. No.31900     10th February 1963     Fed-2

Sat in a corner seat of a compartment coach on a train slowly working from Tonbridge to Redhill in driving snow late on New Year's Eve 1961 we crept past Redhill loco shed. Two 'Schools' class locos were blowing off steam, backlit under the yard lights so their numbers were lost to me. Any thought of 'bunking' the shed were lost in desperation in getting home. However Paul Wells travelled down to Redhill on his NSU Quickly moped and caught No.30901 on the turntable just months before the class was decimated.

Plate 217. No.31410    2nd August 1964    Minolta SR1

Plate 218. No.31868    28th July 1963    Mamiya C22

For me Redhill is forever associated with Southern Moguls and BR Standard '4' tanks working the Redhill to Reading service. The three cylinder Moguls mostly went at the end of 1962 and in Plate 216 No.31900 sits, recently withdrawn, at the rear of Redhill on yet another snowy day. On sunnier occasions two class 'N's No.31868 rests at the rear of the shed whilst No.31410 simmers alongside the depot in August 1964. By December they were were all reallocated to Guildford with some putting in last appearances in the London area.

Plate 219. Norwood Junction Loco Shed       7th July 1963       Mamiya C22

'W' Tanks, July 1963

Plate 220. No.31639       7th July 1963       Mamiya C22

Norwood Junction was always remembered in the late 1950s for twin domed 'C2X' 0-6-0s and 'W' tanks. By the Summer of 1963 the depot was still a stonghold of steam having taken on Stewarts Lane's remaining engines thus giving it, for the first time, passenger diagrams. 'U' class No.31639 presents a fine study 'on shed' but within six months it was all over most had been transferred away, a few remaining until closure in January 1964. Note the diesel shunters, one having the newly introduced diagonal stripes, the other without.

Plate 221.  No.30536        28th July 1963        Mamiya C22

Plate 222.  No.31005        10th February 1963        Fed-2

One of four class 'Q' class engines on shed when visited in July 1963, No.30546 was one of eight allocated here at that time. The old 'H' tanks remained active on the Three Bridges to East Grinstead branch until diesel haulage was introduced in January 1964. No.31005 photographed outside the shed in February 1963 still had seven months to go, but the last two Nos.31263 and 31518, see Plate 379, were withdrawn in January 1964 along with closure of the depot.

Plate 223. No.32353          10th February 1963          Fed-2

'K' class, September 1962
P Wells          Kodak 44A

Plate 224. No.33018          28th July 1963          Mamiya C22

Of 'Brighton' locomotives the 'K' class Moguls were long associated with Three Bridges and outlasted all other types with nine examples being withdrawn from here at the end of 1962. Too late to see them in steam Nos.32353 and 32345 remain in open store early in 1963. Some thirteen class 'Q1' were transferred here in the last year of the depot's life and No.33018 is one of those, with three remaining on the books at closure.

## WILLESDEN

Plate 225. Willesden Loco Shed      11th May 1963      P.Askey - Minolta A5

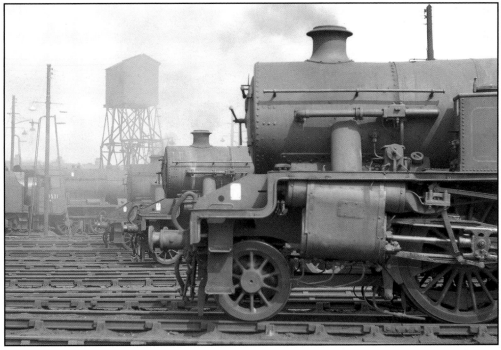

Plate 226. Willesden Loco - Front Ends      27th April 1963      Mamiya C22

For the remainder of this book the chapters will be in locomotive class order due to a lack of engine or location photographs. The Midland Region suffers badly and the Eastern worse. Most trainspotters, including myself were very colloquial in their outlook and a certain degree of favouritism was always present to some regions. Also many pre-1963 Midland negatives have gone missing, including early Home Counties Trips and Willesden's very own LNWR 'G2', unrebuilt 'Patriots' and two stored 'Princesses' outside the roundhouse.

Plate 227. No.40157    17th February 1963    P.Askey - Minolta A5

Plate 228. No.42336    11th May 1963    P.Askey - Minolta A5

If Old Oak Common was to become our 'home from home' then naturally Willesden, a five minute walk away was our second home, but not so welcoming as its Western neighbour. Unlike Old Oak depot Willesden never became a major dumping ground for stored locos and the Stanier '3MT', No.40157 was already suffering from vandalism and was one of the last of the class to be withdrawn. However parallel boiler Fowler tank, No.42336, was one of the earlier examples of this class to go, and both are stored up at the top end of the yard. They did not linger long.

# FAIRBURN & STANIER LARGE TANKS

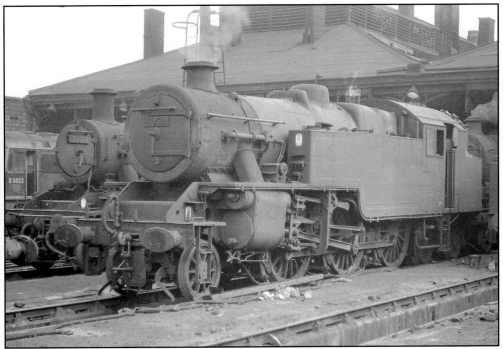

Plate 229. No.42080        24th January 1965        Minolta SR1

Plate 230. No.42573        16th August 1964        Minolta SR1

Detail differences are apparent in these two views of Fairburn and Stanier large tanks, both photographs taken at Willesden. The Fairburn version, No.42080, was a post-war improvement on Stanier's original pre-war design as shown in No.42573. As can be seen, towards the end of their working lives loco depots deteriorated with rubbish and debris cluttering the place and diesels having to share space with their grimy neighbours. The large tanks were kept busy on ECS duties until July 1965 when they were put into store following removal of watering facilities from Euston.

# LMS MOGULS

Plate 231. No.42815          16th August 1964          Minolta SR1

Plate 232. No.43021          15th September 1963          P.Askey - Minolta A5

Again a certain difference in style is noticeable between Hughes 1926 design better known as 'Crabs' and unusual at that time with its very high running plate. Ivatt's post-war version has more than a little in common with the later BR Standard classes. Both photographs are at Willesden and whilst the 'Crabs' were common enough with No.42815 positioned outside the Roundhouse the Ivatt locos were uncommon and No.43021 is undergoing repairs inside Willesden's Victorian built workshops.

Plate 233.  No.43645                    2nd March 1963                    Fed-2

Plate 234.  No.44422                    31st January 1965                    Minolta SR1

Something to bore your average 1960s trainspotter to tears. Whilst the early Midland '3F' class as shown here by No.43645 out of steam at Gloucester Barnwood has some charm, the same cannot be said for the LMS '4F' version. However No.44422 seen here in January 1965 at Gloucester (Horton Road) from a passing train has been reduced to a 0-4-0 configuration This loco was allocated to the Somerset & Dorset and was not withdrawn until June 1965, so whether it returned home or was slowly working its way to Barry dump and preservation I do not know.

# 'BLACK 5s'

Plate 235. No.44946        circ. 1963/64        P.Wells - Kodak 44A

Plate 236. No.45409        16th August 1964        Minolta SR1

Always glad to see a 'Black 5' but with well over eight hundred of them around they could become somewhat repetitive, and Willesden had its fair share with a dozen or so still there at closure. Paul's photo of No.44946 has, I believe, just returned from breakdown duties. By the 1960s the obligatory push bike racks were becoming empty as railway workers took to the car, and with little or no parking at hand they could be seen dumped all over the place. Love the big black Vauxhall, we brought one second hand a few years later for £25.

Plate 237. No.45528 *R.E.M.E*        17th February 1963        Fed-2

Plate 238. No.45566 *Nova Scotia*        27th April 1963        Mamiya C22

Introduced in 1930 the first two were 'rebuilds' of LNWR 'Claughtons' and all were originally built with parallel boilers with some, as pictured, being rebuilt with taper boilers and detail differences. No.45528 lies out of steam in Willesden Roundhouse shortly after withdrawal, she did not linger and was soon gone. Although No.45556 is a 'Jubilee' surrounded by 'Britannias' at Willesden depot, she was one of the last batch ordered as 'Patriots' but instead were built with taper boilers etc by Stanier and became the first of the 'Jubilees'.

Plate 239.  No.45622 *Nyasaland*                    25th May 1963                    P.Askey - Minolta A5

Plate 240.  No.45735 *Comet*                    6th April 1963                    P.Askey - Minolta A5

Following on from the 'Patriots' the 'Jubilees' were introduced in 1934 and two of them were rebuilt in 1942 with larger taper boilers similar to the rebuilt 'Royal Scots'. Wembley Cup Final day in 1963 was the 25th May and despite many football specials being diesel hauled, Cricklewood depot managed eight 'Jubilees' on shed and No.45622 was one of them. No.45735 was one of the two 'Jubilee' rebuilds and they were near indistinguishable from the 'Royal Scots', however both were withdrawn early in September 1964

Plate 241.  No.46101 *Royal Scots Grey*      15th September 1963      Mamiya C22

Plate 242.  No.46115 *Scots Guardsman*      25th May 1963      P.Askey - Minolta A5

Ordered straight from the drawing board by Fowler in the late 1920s with parallel boilers they were all rebuilt by Stanier with taper boiler and other detail differences by 1955, withdrawals commenced seven years later. Some twenty of the class found themselves allocated to Willesden during the 1960s and No.46101 is pictured outside Willesden Roundhouse having just been withdrawn with a suspected cracked right hand cylinder. As per the previous page the 'Royal Scots' contribution to Cup Final day at Cricklewood was the solitary example of No.46115.

Plate 243.  No.46240 *City of Coventry*     7th July 1963                    Mamiya C22

Plate 244.  No.46256 *Sir William A Stanier FRS*    10th August 1962       P.Wells Kodak 44A

Just how the LMS could produce mind numbing things such as 'Jinty' tanks and '4Fs', send you to sleep with the ubiquitous 'Back 5s' and '8Fs' yet come out with the 'Coronations' is beyond belief. Built over an eleven year period the majority of the early builds were streamliners, the last coming into service in 1948 one year before the last streamliner was rebuilt. Camden, in the late 1950s, seemed to exude express classes to the exclusion of all other types. With dieselisation from the early 1960s steam was quickly in decline and Camden became fully dieselised in September 1963, its last three 'Coronations' being transferred to Willesden.

Plate 245. No.46239 *City of Chester*          7th July 1963          P.Askey - Minolta A5

Plate 246. No.46239 *City of Chester*          15th September 1963          Mamiya C22

Of Camden's last three 'Coronations' Nos.46240 & 46239 (Plates 243/5) are on shed with only two months before the end of steam. By this time Camden was home to English Electric 'Type 4s' and the depot would suffer the further indignity of partial demolition before final closure in 1966. Willesden, built in 1873 to take the burden of freight locomotives away from Camden, finally took on the mantle of main line operations from Camden some ninety years later. And so, for a short period, Willesden experienced an Indian Summer of express steam just prior to final closure in 1965.

Plate 247. No.46245 *City of London*       15th September 1963       Mamiya C22

Plate 248. No.45248 *City of Leeds*       26th January 1964       Mamiya C22

Camden's other last was 'Coronation' No.46245 photographed in Willesden's 1930 built roundhouse. No.46245 was the last 'Coronation' to receive a general overhaul in October 1962 and was always kept in excellent condition. Visits to Willesden during 1963 could produce 'Coronations', 'Royal Scots', 'Patriots', 'Jubilees' and 'Britannias' running into double figures. My last photograph of a 'Coronation' was No.46248 storming out of the roundhouse and running past the straight shed on a misty day in January 1964, nine months later they had all gone.

Plate 249. No.46250 *City of Litchfield*    15th September 1963    Mamiya C22

Plate 250. No.46251 *City of Nottingham*    6th April 1963    Mamiya C22

Late built 'Coronations' Nos.46250 and 46251 in Willesden's shed yard showing front end differences to the earlier locomotives, although the penultimate build No.46256 (Plate 244) shows differences again. During 1963 the 'Coronations' were kept busy with diesel shortages, relief duties, parcel and stand-by workings and this kept them going through 1964, but the 'Coro's swansong must have been the Grand National specials to Aintree with six being prepared. Willesden's only allocated 'Coronations' were those from Camden and these were transferred away in August 1964.

# 'JINTY' TANKS

Plate 251.  No.47500                16th August 1964                Minolta SR1

Plate 252.  No.47501                16th August 1964                Minolta SR1

Although not so numerous as the Western panniers, but just like them, every former LMS depot seemed to have some and Willesden was no exception. Of the two photographs No.47500 is a stranger and rests outside the workshops with its middle wheel set missing whilst No.47501, one of Wiillesden's very own, is parked up outside the shed alongside the Grand Union canal. Local coal train workings were their last duties and this finished in July 1965 . It is believed that 'Jinty' No.47432 had the honour to be the last steam loco to leave the site in November 1965.

Plate 253. No.48193                16th August 1964                Minolta SR1

Plate 254. No.48531                24th January 1965                Minolta SR1

These played a large part in freight traffic and fifteen of them were still on the books at Willesden on closure. Of the two examples shown neither were built by the LMS, No.48193 was a North British locomotive and one of the last to go in 1968. Meanwhile No.48531 was a Doncaster built LNER loco which transferred to the LMS in 1946. Again the bottom photo shows the mess that Willesden was getting into towards the end, something you would not have seen earlier. I do love the spring left in the ash pit.

Plate 255.  No.70010 *Owen Glendower*        16th August 1964                                    Minolta SR1

Plate 256.  No.70014 *Iron Duke*        16th August 1964                                    Minolta SR1

With steam giving way to diesel across the board, express class locomotives found themselves on lesser routes and by September 1961 the Great Central took on Midland Region 'Britannias' working Nottingham semi-fasts. These GC diagrams came to Willesden in late 1962 and further classmates arrived in April 1963 from the Eastern Region. From then on up to a dozen could be seen on shed until transferred away early in 1965. No.70014, now past its best, was once one of Stewarts Lane's finest, working the 'Golden Arrow' Pullman service only seven years previous.

Plate 257. No.78043        c.1963        Paul Wells Kodak 44A

Plate 258. No.92022        16th August 1964        Minolta SR1

Few other BR Standard types found themselves allocated to Willesden other than Standard class '2' 2-6-0s and No.78043 is one of fifteen which were allocated at Willesden from 1963 onwards. These found themselves on a multitude of tasks including ECS duties at Euston. Of the '9Fs' very few were allocated or seen and former Franco-Crosti boilered '8F' No.92022 is waiting to be coaled up. Ten such locomotives were built but the experiment was not deemed successful and they were rebuilt by the early 1960s, but classified 8F due to having smaller boilers than standard.

## 'A3' PACIFIC No.60085 *MANNA*

Plate 259. No.60085 *Manna*          7th July 1963          Mamiya C22

Plate 260. No.60085 *Manna*          7th July 1963          Mamiya C22

The Eastern Region was largely ignored by us all. Trainspotting in the late 1950s always took in Kings Cross, Hornsey, Stratford, etc but with no camera. On a rare camera toting visit to Stratford I could not understand why it resulted in only three negatives until reading the film numbers 34, 35 and 36. Hence two photographs of No.60085 on Kings Cross depot, July 1963, one month after closure. She was the only occupant. The last scheduled steam ran some two weeks later, the last actual steam working over a year later. Coaling facilities were withdrawn, then restored. The replacement of steam with diesel was a contracted affair.

## EARLY DIESEL & ELECTRIC LOCOMOTIVES

Plate 261.  No.10001                    17th February 1963                    P.Askey - Minolta A5

Plate 262.  No.20001                    7th July 1963                    Mamiya C22

Both prototypes, No.10001 is photographed at Willesden with steam still two years to go. Built by the LMS in 1947 she and her sister engine performed express work, sometimes in tandem, but were later relegated to secondary duties, withdrawal came in 1966. The Southern Railway took an electric approach and No.20001 is caught here outside her home depot of Stewarts Lane. Note the air raid shelter sign and shelter under the railway arch. A class of three they were built from 1941 onwards. All were withdrawn in 1968. The footbridge entrance to Stewarts Lane loco shed can just be glimpsed on the left of the bottom photograph.

# DIESEL ELECTRIC & HYDRAULIC LOCOMOTIVES

Plate 263.  No.D307                    24th January 1965                    Minolta SR1

Plate 264.  No.D604 *Cossack*                    7th January 1961                    Kodak620

The English Electric 'Type 4s' were introduced in 1958, the majority being constructed by Vulcan Foundry, however No.D307 pictured here at Willesden was one of twenty built by Robert Stephenson & Hawthorn. The class was soon working out of Euston operating from Camden depot but few were seen on Wlillesden until 1964. The North British built diesel hydraulics were the first to see service on the Western Region in 1958 and No.D604 is positioned outside Old Oak Common workshops with rails run across the traverser pit which had just been removed. Inset: The same loco at Swindon Works in May 1963.

Plate 265.  No.D800 *Sir Brian Robertson*        6th October 1962        Fed -2

Plate 266.  No.D815 *Druid*        16th August 1964        Minolta SR1

The first D800s were Swindon built and based on the German Federal Railway's class 'V200', powered by two high revving Maybach engines each running through a hydraulic transmission system. Later locomotives were North British built and MAN engined. They were small locos and very light, weighing in at eighty tons, and were always allocated to West Country depots. Old Oak Common steam shed always played host to diesels (Plates 268 and 270) whilst the workshops were partially converted for diesel maintenance purposes in 1960. By 1962 the carriage sheds, which housed the Western Pullman sets, were put over for diesel locomotive use.

# THE 'WARSHIPS'

Plate 267. No.D825 *Intrepid*    6th September 1964                    Minolta SR1

Plate 268. No.D843 *Sharpshooter*    7th March 1964                    Mamiya C22

In early 1959 they started to make an impact and by the Summer of 1959 the Western Region Civil Engineer had introduced a 95mph restriction on the class. I remember being pulled back to Swindon from Bristol with great excitement at the platform end when the crew related we had been travelling at over 100mph. Being a latter day 'Rocker' it amused me that I had first done the 'ton' on a train. Plates 265 and 266 illustrate Nos.D800 and D815 in Old Oak's former carriage shop, with D800 showing disc indicators, as fitted to the first twelve locos, but later modified with a two piece routebox.

# THE 'WARSHIPS'

Plate 269.  No.D847 *Strongbow*                   5th July 1964                   Minolta SR1

Plate 270.  No.D861 *Vigilant*                   7th June 1964                   Minolta SR1

Regional boundary changes in January 1963 meant the Western took over the Southern main line west of Salisbury and by the Summer of 1964 the 'Warships' appeared to replace steam. A travel worn No.D825 (Plate 267) is on Exmouth Junction in September 1964 at a time when the old Southern main line was truncated at Exeter and the service downgraded. After initial successes the 'Warships' suffered problems and the whole class was withdrawn between 1968 and 1972. The photo of No.D847 (Plate 269) outside Swindon 'C' Shop is a bit premature, she was cut up there, but some nine years later.

Plate 271. No.D1007 *Western Talisman*  2nd September 1962  Fed-2

Plate 272. No.D1009 *Western Invader*  26th August 1962  Fed-2

More powerful than the 'Warships' they were built at Swindon and Crewe and were initially allocated to Plymouth (Laira) during 1962. By the end of the year the majority were allocated to Old Oak Common (Plates 273 and 274), in part, to replace steam on the Wolverhampton service. They appeared in June 1962 precipitating full scale dieselisation for the Winter timetable. By late 1962 they were allocated to Cardiff Canton to take over the South Wales services from the underpowered 'Hymeks' which was achieved during 1963. As I recall, none of this went smoothly.

Plate 273. No.D1023 *Western Fusilier*    11th April 1964    Mamiya C22

Plate 274. No.D1037 *Western Empress*    25th July 1964    Minolta SR1

Sadly very little went smoothly on the transition from steam to diesel and the 'Westerns' were no exception, it was reported that in late 1963 fifty percent of the 'Westerns' were out of service. The 'Westerns' did not stay long on the Wolverhampton roster and by the Spring of 1964 the service was completely in the hands of the Brush-Sulzer diesel electrics. By this time Old Oak Common's own allocation of 'Westerns' dropped dramatically and by the end of 1965 they had been transferred away and would never be allocated there again.

Plate 275.  No.D1040 *Western Queen*          29th September 1962          Fed-2

Plate 276.  No.D1044 *Western Duchess*          12th August 1962          Fed-2

The murky conditions that diesels had to put up with can clearly be seen in some of the photographs. Maintenance must have been problematic in the early days and Old Oak Common had some facilities in the former carriage sheds (Plates 271 and 276) or the modernised former steam workshops, but many had to share space in the steam locomotive sheds (Plate 278). Meanwhile Cardiff Canton's diesels were being serviced in the old carriage sheds which had been originally adapted for DMU use before the former steam depot was demolished and rebuilt and the site redeveloped.

# THE 'WESTERNS'

Plate 277. No.D1048 *Western Lady*        5th July 1964        Minolta SR1

Plate 278. No.D1051 *Western Ambassador*        22nd February 1964        Mamiya C22

Plate 275 shows No.D1040 at Old Oak Common ex-works from Crewe in immaculate maroon livery without the front end yellow warning panel. These started to appear throughout 1962 and perhaps Mo.D1040 was one of the last not so treated. On a 1962 Swindon Works visit No.D1009 (Plate 272) is the latest build and others up to No.D1024 were under construction. By the time of our visit in 1964 'Western' construction was complete and Crewe built No.D1048 (Plate 277) stands proudly outside 'A' Shop. Some thirteen years later she would be one of the last to be withdrawn after a relatively short working life.

Plate 279. Old Oak Common's original diesel depot  24th January 1965                    Minolta SR1

Plate 280.  No.D1717                    22nd February 1964                    Mamiya C22

The Western Region of British Railways had led a independent existence since Nationalisation and this resulted in developing diesel hydraulic as opposed to diesel electric traction. Be it politics or locomotive transmission problems, by the early sixties a decision had been made to abandon diesel hydraulic locomotives. Newly built Brush-Sulzer No.D1500 was therefore transferred to Swindon in September 1962 for trials, and by October 1963 transfers began to Old Oak Common to replace the 'Western' class on the Paddington Wolverhampton service.

Plate 281. No.D1727          11th April 1964          Mamiya C22

Plate 282. No.D1733          16th August 1964          Minolta SR1

The diesel electrics soon became established, as the four views at Old Oak Common show. On our last visit to Old Oak in early 1965 Plate 279 clearly shows the impact of the diesel electrics in the former carriage sheds. However a feeling of improvisation clearly shows with oil drums, home made dexion platforms and trolley bench nicked from the steam shed scattered around. Just outside, some months earlier, another Brush locomotive No.D1733 appeared in overall blue. It was apparently, so we were informed, a trial livery for locomotive and train to be called XP64. A portent for BR's blue and grey period.

Plate 283.  Tonbridge Locomotive Shed          2nd August 1964          Minolta SR1

Plate 284.  No.D6571          2nd August 1964          Minolta SR1

One of the more successful types of BR's Modernisation Plan. First delivered in 1960 they were allocated entirely on the Southern Region, initially to Hither Green then Eastleigh, but could be found all over the system. No.D6571 with other members of the class had taken over most of Brighton depot's steam duties by the Summer of 1963 but initial problems meant they did not eliminate steam until 1965. Likewise Tonbridge, by late 1964, was predominantly diesel, but steam hung on until closure in January 1965, the depot site being used as a diesel signing on point for many years.

Plate 285. No.D6822        21st June 1964        Minolta SR1

Plate 286. No.D6827        25th July 1964        Minolta SR1

Introduced in 1960 this class commenced trials on the Western Region in September 1962 in South Wales and by early 1963 were working mineral trains up the valleys. Rapid deliveries meant that within a year they could cover all freight diagrams in South Wales, working some duties in pairs. By June 1964 over fifty were allocated to Cardiff Canton and nearly seventy to Swansea Landore. Although none were ever allocated to Newport Ebbw, No.D6822, is one of twenty on shed on 21st June 1964, whilst at the London end No.D6827 records the only time I ever witnessed the class on Old Oak Common.

Plate 287.  No.D7049                  6th October 1962                  Fed-2

Plate 288.  Nos.D7050 & D1010          23nd February 1964          Mamiya C22

The most successful of the diesel hydraulics, Maybach powered, and introduced in 1961, 'Hymeks' commenced working the South Wales services in early 1962 and started taking over the Western Region's last steam stamping ground, the Hereford and Worcester, services in May 1963. They were deemed underpowered on the South Wales route and were replaced by the more powerful 'Western' class in late 1963, by which time they commanded the Hereford and Worcester services.

# BEYER PEACOCK 'HYMEK' CLASS

Plate 289. No.D7063            7th March 1964            Mamiya C22

Plate 290. No.D7069            23rd February 1964            Mamiya C22

Deliveries were completed by 1964 by which time they were spread across the Western Region with the majority of the class allocated to Bristol. Nos.D7049 (Plate 287) and D7063 were photographed at Old Oak with D7063 within the confines of the steam shed and is something of a culture shock against the crudity of steam age technology. The tool boxes on the workbench no doubt come from old long gone pannier tanks. In Plate 288 at Taunton, No.D7050 has to share with steam a little longer but No.D7069 is at Exeter where the depot closed to steam some five months earlier and is now reduced to a diesel signing on point.

# NORTH BRITISH TYPE 2

Plate 291. No.D6320    6th September 1962    Minolta SR1

Plate 292. No.D6326    7th March 1964    Mamiya C22

One of the earlier diesel types put into production before proper evaluation. Introduced in 1959 and built by the North British Company they were allocated to Cornwall and Devon which was the Western Region's initial area for dieselisation. They remained in the West Country allocated between Newton Abbot and Laira, with No.D6320 seen at Exmouth Junction, but some found their way to Old Oak Common on ECS duties of which No.D6326 was the first allocated in late 1963. All had been withdrawn by 1972.

Plate 293. No.D9503                    5th July 1964                    Minolta SR1

Plate 294. No.D9500                    5th July 1964                    Minolta SR1

These were the last of the Western Region's diesel hydraulics, built between 1964/5. I have always understood this be a class that never should have been built. They were designed for transfer freights etc, but this was a type of traffic that was rapidly coming to an end when the class was being built. The two photographs were taken on the same day at Swindon Works with No.D9500 residing in the weighhouse whilst No.D9504 is one of sixteen under construction in 'A' Shop. They were scrapped or sold to industry between 1967 and 1969, both the above going to the National Coal Board.

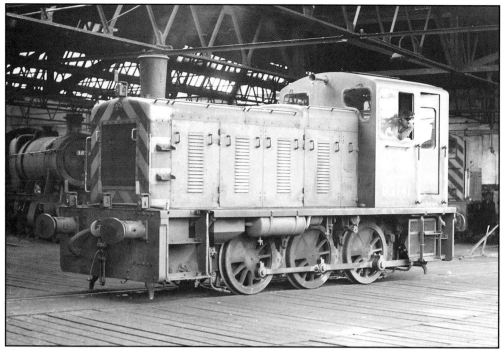

Plate 295. No.D2141            6th September 1964            Minolta SR1

Plate 296. Nos.D2180/D2146        .        5th July 1964            Minolta SR1

Introduced between 1957 and 1962. No.D2141, a Taunton loco, had just rolled into the shed and positioned itself on the turntable. She was one of four allocated there at that time. Nos.D2180 and D2146 are photographed at Swindon depot from a passing train. D2180 was a Bournemouth engine and possibly in for repairs whilst D2146 was one of Swindon's own, but in March 1965 had her cab cut down for working on the BP&GR line in South Wales. Whilst Nos.D2141 and D2180 eventually became class '03' under TOPS, No.D2146 had been withdrawn by 1968 and scrapped.

Plate 297. No.D2279       5th April 1964       Mamiya C22

Plate 298. No.D2518       24th January 1965       Minolta SR1

The Drewry shunters were introduced between 1952 and 1961. Allocated to Norwood Junction but caught here shunting at Stewarts Lane carriage sheds just alongside the former Longhedge Locomotive Works, No.D2279 was one of the last to be withdrawn in 1971. The prototype of this class was Hither Green's No.DS1173 which was built back in 1947. No.D2518, photographed inside Willesden Roundhouse, was one of ten engines built by Hudswell Clarke in 1961. It was the only example I ever saw there. Two years later the whole class had been sold or scrapped, this particular loco being sold on to the NCB.

Plate 299. No.12090        24th January 1965        Minolta SR1

Plate 300. No.15100        3rd February 1963        P.Askey - Minolta A5

No.12090, pictured in Willesden shed yard, was one of many built by the English Electric Company for the LMS. Built between 1944 and 1952 this particular example being a latter day BR example. There were always a few poking around Willesden. This loco was withdrawn in 1971, the final few examples going in 1972. No.15100 was another English Electric engine built for the GWR in 1935, six more following in 1946. Seen at Southall depot, with an apparently built on water column, this locomotive had the experimental safety wasp stripes applied in the 1950s, and was withdrawn in 1965.

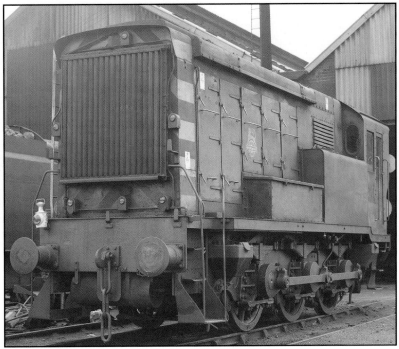

Plate 301. No.15201        29th September 1963        Mamiya C22

Plate 302. No.15223        21st July 1963        Mamiya C22

No.15201 was a Southern Railway example, built at Ashford Works in 1937 with an English Electric engine as Southern Railway No.1. It was photographed at Eastleigh following transfer from Norwood Junction and was withdrawn the following year, transferring into Departmental stock and being cut up in the early 1970s. No.15223, seen at Feltham, was of BR construction the class being built between 1949-51. They were noted for their 'box-pok' wheels. Never allocated to Feltham, this was the only example I ever saw there. It was one of the first to go in 1969, the class was extinct by 1971.

## STEAM LOCOMOTIVE DUMPS

Plate 303.  Old Oak Common                2nd September 1962                Fed-2

Plate 304.  Old Oak Common               16th June 1963               P.Askey - Minolta A5

Locomotive dumps such as the one pictured at Old Oak Common, above, were generally unknown to me until 1962. On our tours of London Motive Power Depots in 1959, only Nine Elms stands out, with many interesting locos dumped in the shed yard following the Eastern Section electrification. Most depots had their 'dead' engines, generally with their chimneys sacked over. Willesden had a LNWR 'G2' and a few Fowler tanks, an old '2F' 0-6-0 lived at Cricklewood. Neasden had a line of 'N5' tanks, and Brighton had two beautiful class 'L' 4-4-0s.

Plate 305. Old Oak Common         26th August 1962         Fed-2

Plate 306. Old Oak Common         12th August 1962         Fed-2

Year's end 1961, two 'Princess' Pacifics were stored outside Willesden Roundhouse and by the Summer of 1962 a handful of 'Kings', 'Castles' and panniers formed a orderly queue at Old Oak. By September twenty five locos were stored. Plate 305 finds an overflow alongside the Grand Union canal comprising Nos.6019/26/9/5008/36. At this stage chimneys were no longer sacked over, everyone knew they were not going anywhere, and the name and number plates had just been removed. Plans were hatched to 'rescue' a 'King' nameplate but came to nothing.

Plate 307. Southall        7th June 1964        Minolta SR1

Plate 308. Southall        7th June 1964        Minolta SR1

August 1962 found Nos.7020, 6025 and 6028 (Plate 306) stored in the former carriage sheds as reserve locomotives for excessive diesel failures - well that's what they told us. The 'Kings' were not withdrawn until year's end, so it could have been so, but I don't think they ever turned a wheel. The extensive yards at Southall depot held many dumped engines by June 1964 and this included 'King' No.6028 ex-Old Oak (Plate 307 - middle row). This lot were cleared within weeks of these photos being taken, with No.6028 being the last stored 'King' to go from the London area.

# STEAM LOCOMOTIVE DUMPS

Plate 356. Severn Tunnel Junction        12th July 1964        Minolta SR1

Plate 310. Newport (Ebbw Junction)       14th October 1962       Fed-2

By 1962 onwards most Western depots had lines of stored engines, some waiting over a year before finally being towed off for scrap. Generally by 1963 name and number plates had been removed, but as time went on it could be difficult to ascertain if locos were quite finished with. As the numbers of withdrawn locomotives increased separate dumps were made up. Plate 356 shows Severn Tunnel Junction with a Southern interloper on its way to South Wales, whilst on a misty day at Newport a dump had been formed alongside Ebbw depot.

Plate 311. Swindon Works          26th August 1962          Fed-2

Plate 312. Swindon Works          26th August 1962          Fed-2

Swindon Works visits were always full of interest but in August 1962 it became clear that it was all up for steam. The 'Kings' and 'Castles' not only resided on the dump but up to a dozen were lined up tender-less alongside 'A' Shop. We were told that the safety valve covers and name and number plates were being removed that week. The two 'Kings', withdrawn in June, had been in store at Cardiff Canton whilst the 'Castles' had all been withdrawn in May and none would see the next year. By November the two 'Kings' Nos.6023 and 6024 were on the dump, but that turned out to be another story.

Plate 313. No.7798 and others     15th October 1961          Kodak44A

Plate 314. General view Swindon dump          26th May 1963          Mamiya C22

Scrap yards have always had a great fascination for me, even the yards feeding the foundries that I worked for. Railway plates and motor cycle engines have been rescued from such places by myself, lately to be sold for great financial gain. Swindon dump was no exception and I have been fascinated by photographs from the end of broad gauge onwards. What comes to mind, on one visit, was a large pile of cast number plates all smashed in half, obviously no one to 'rescue' them then. By early 1965 scrapping had ceased, preserved locos Nos.1442, 2818 and 6412 hung about for months, but by year's end the dump was empty.

# THE 'KINGS'

Plate 315.  No.6021 (w/d Sept '62)          29th September 1962                    Fed-2

Plate 316.  No.6026 (w/d Sept '62)          29th September 1962                    Fed-2

Of all the four Regions classic express locomotives, the Great Western 'Kings' were the first to go, the whole class being withdrawn in 1962. The first to go No.6006 was noted, withdrawn, at Swindon in March 1962. By June 1962 Nos.6020/29 were stored outside Old Oak Common's workshops and by September they had been joined by Nos.6009/10/19/21/25/26/28 and no less than fourteen 'Castles'. No.6005 joined the ranks in November. Four still remained there by 1963 including No.6010 which had 'lost' the copper capping to its chimney some months previous.

# THE 'KINGS'

No.6004 on Swindon dump, August 1962

Plate 317. No.6027 (w/d Sept '62)     23rd September 1962     Fed-2

Plate 318. No.6012 (w/d Sept '62)     23rd September 1962     Fed-2

'Kings' recorded stored at Cardiff Canton were Nos.6003/4//23/24 whilst Wolverhampton (Stafford Road) held Nos.6001/2/7/12/14/15/17/22. However some landed up in odd places, Didcot had No.6011, Leamington Spa held No.6016 and Banbury No.6027. This locomotive, when photographed, so I was told had recently failed and been put off at Banbury, hence chimney 'sacked' and work being done on the inner cylinders. To no avail she was withdrawn that month but was still at Banbury in April 1963. Whatever, by June 1963 she had been cut up at Swindon .

Plate 319. Nos.5033 (w/d Sept '62) & 5960(w/d Sept '62)     2nd December 1962     Fed-2

No.5069 Swindon dump, March 1962

Plate 320. No.5038 (w/d Sept '63)     23rd February 1964     Mamiya C22

No.5069, Swindon dump March 1962, the first time I ever saw a 'Castle' for scrap. I have a somewhat under exposed negative of it, you can just read 'engine not scrap' on a somewhat nibbled cab. She was one of the early ones to go but within a matter of months dumped 'Castles' became common place everywhere. Oxford depot holds No.5033 on a cold misty evening, note the frost on the 'Hall's tender, she had been there two months earlier and according to 'records' had already been scrapped. Meanwhile No.5038 forms part of a scrap train at Reading depot.

# THE 'HALLS'

Plate 321. No.4984(w/d Sept '62)     14th October 1962     Fed-2

Plate 322. No.5901(w/d June '64)     12th July 1964     Minolta SR1

The 'Hall' class comprised some 258 locomotives, but it was not until 1962 that any serious inroads were made. One of these was No.4984 looking down from the coaler at Cardiff (East Dock). Although just withdrawn, we met up again at R S Hayes yard, Bridgend in July 1964, the month she was scrapped. A few years earlier John and Hayley Mills were running round Cardiff Docks filming 'Tiger Bay', or was it Newport Docks . . . or Barry Docks? Worth buying the DVD, lots of outside location work, including a glimpse of a half cab pannier.

# THE 'HALLS'

Plate 323. Nos.6930(w/d Oct '65) & 2841(w/d Dec '63)    23rd July 1964                    Minolta  SR1

Plate 324. No.6970 (w/d June '64)          19th July 1964                    Minolta  SR1

In Plate 322 'Hall' No.5901 finds itself in the company of 'Castle' No.5039 and others outside the repair shops alongside the Bristol main line at Reading depot. Southall dump had been cleared when the shot at the top of this page was taken in July 1964, but within months had restocked. Note the large AEC sign, a company well known for its buses and lorries, this huge sprawling complex was rail connected but has now gone. 'Modified Hall' No.6970 awaits her fate at Oxford depot, the covered van alongside giving the photograph a railway preservation feel to it.

Plate 325.  No.1027(w/d Oct '63)          2nd February 1964          Mamiya C22

Plate 326.  No.7825 (w/d May '64)          19th July 1964          Minolta SR1

Swindon depot always had a problem holding stored locomotives, with the Stock Shed and Gas Works becoming full. By 1963/4 things were getting crowded and on this February 1964 visit 'County' No.1027 finds herself alongside the shed itself with four of the few remaining active classmates tucked away in the loco shed. The 'Manors' were rare in the London area until several were allocated to Reading. Two were in store by the Summer of 1964. If proof was needed that my images are unaltered who else would leave a signal post sticking out of a chimney pot?

# THE 'GRANGES'

Plate 327. No.6818 (w/d April '64)          21st June 1964          Minolta SR1

Plate 328. No.6824 (w/d April '64)          5th July 1964          Minolta SR1

The 'Granges' really held together only suffering major withdrawals towards the end of Western Region steam, the last ones going, as did all other GW tender locos, in December 1965. Fairly common in the London Division when in steam, few were seen out of service. Both locomotives featured here were withdrawn in April 1964, No.6818 at Newport Ebbw has lost its number plate and safety valve cover but still retains its nameplate. Perhaps not 'rescued' yet. No.6824 stands on Swindon dump in front of long turn dump resident 'King' No.6010, the last one scrapped in September 1965. No.6824 lasted until November 1964.

Plate 329. No.2862 (w/d April '64)     21st June 1964     Minolta SR1

Plate 330. No.2875 (w/d April '64)     21st June 1964     Minolta SR1

The Great Western's all time freight locomotive built over a forty year span from 1903. In two classes, the earlier '2800' followed by the '2884' class Apparently preferred by engine crews to all others with the last ones going in 1965. The two represented here are from the earlier build, were both withdrawn in April 1964 and apparently both cut up in February 1965. No.2862 and others at Severn Tunnel Junction were having their tenders emptied of coal whilst No.2875 has for a backdrop the imposing Cardiff Bute Street Victorian Dock offices. And still there in 2010.

Plate 331. Nos.6367 (w/d Nov '64) & 6317 (w/d Nov '63)   23rd September 1962                    Fed-2

Plate 332. No.6302 (w/d March '62)          26th August 1962                                        Fed-2

With Banbury depot in the background you could be excused for thinking that time's up for these two Western Moguls. Chimneys are sacked over for good reason, these two will live to fight another day. The photograph dates from September 1962 but No.6367 moves on to Didcot and is to be one of the last to be withdraw, in November 1964. Classmate No.6317, less its smoke box number plate, survives until November 1963. Swindon dump, August 1962, has a trio of Moguls, Nos.6302, 7334 and 6348 all withdrawn in early 1962 but will happily rust away into the new year.

# '2251' CLASS

Plate 333. No.2201 (w/d June '64)          5th July 1964                    Minolta SR1

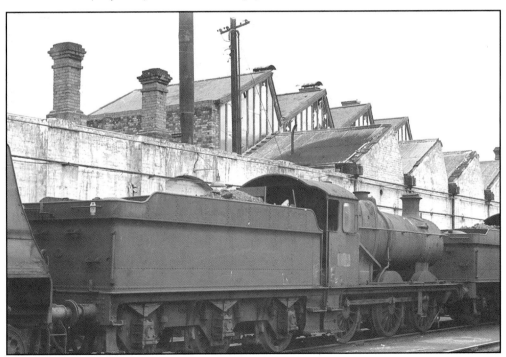

Plate 334. No.2214 (w/d May '65)          6th September 1964              Minolta SR1

Referred to as the '2251' class because that was the numbered series of the first batch from 1930, reverting to 2200 etc from 1938 onwards. No 2201 was allocated to Reading depot in January 1964 but was withdrawn in June. The repair shop behind holds No.2899, just poking its nose through the open door. Of more interest is No.2214 transferred to Exmouth Junction, now Western Region, in August 1963 and finally withdrawn from that depot in May 1965, but as you can see, is stored at Exeter in September 1964. Plenty of coal in the tender though, she was actually one of the last to be cut up in August 1965.

Plate 335.  No.4282 (w/d Sept '63)          12th July 1964                    Minolta SR1

Plate 336.  No.4293 (w/d Aug '62)          26th August 1962                  Fed-2

Staple diet for all freight workings up and down the South Wales valleys. Introduced in 1910 with 200 built over the next thirty years, with many rebuilt into the larger '72xx' class during the 1930s. No.4282 was photographed during our uninvited visit to R S Hayes yard, Bridgend, a surprisingly friendly establishment with no nice doggies to worry about! Meanwhile on a conducted tour around Swindon Works and dump in August 1962 we see No.4293 and our long-suffering tour guides, no doubt sad to see there long respected 'Kings' on the scrap heap and young men when they were built.

# LARGE PRAIRIE TANKS - '5101' & REBUILDS

Plate 337. No.5187 (w/d May '62)　　　26th August 1962　　　Fed-2

Plate 338. No.8102 (w/d May '64)　　　5th July 1964　　　Minolta SR1

The Great Western had a long history of using Prairie tanks, the '5101' class being in part rebuilds of an earlier '31xx' class, with latter build new engines. No.5187 was a new build and on Swindon dump in August 1962, being withdrawn in May and scrapped by October. The '81xx' class were the last of large Prairies to be built in 1939. In actual fact they were rebuilds of the '5101' class. No.8102 appears outside Swindon 'A' Shop looking like a spares ship, perhaps keeping the remainder of the class running. She was scrapped in August 1964.

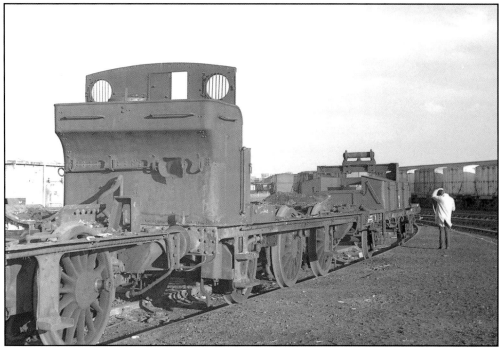

Plate 339. No.7799 (w/d May '62)          16th December 1962          Fed-2

Plate 340. No.9456 (w/d April '64)          21st June 1964          Minolta SR1

Not a lot left in these two views. '57xx' class No.7799 on Swindon dump is reduced to a set of wheels and frames with a couple of crane jib carriers for scrap. It looks to be a windy day judging by the railway enthusiast, either that or last night's curry has blown his head off and his backside away. Did we eat curries in the sixties? Class '94xx' No.9456 seems to be in a state at Cardiff East Dock having lost its panniers into the nearby wagon. Whether much more went into the wagon I do not know, she was withdrawn in May 1964 and gone by October.

Plate 341. No.1143 (w/d Nov '60)  19th February 1961  Kodak 620 Box Camera

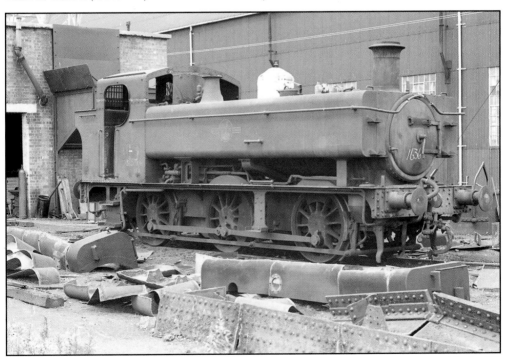

Plate 342. No.1636 (w/d June '64)  5th July 1964  Minolta SR1

Keen to catch the little Peckett saddle tanks around Swansea Docks, a Home Counties trip in September 1960 found Nos.1151, 1152, and 1338 at Swansea East Dock. Danygraig, a distinctive castle like depot featured in endless 1950s Ian Allen 'ABCs' was devoid of steam and populated with small diesel mechanicals. All that was left by the time Ted owned a camera was the cut up remains of No.1143 at Caerphilly Works in February 1961. No.1636 was one of four '16xx' panniers littered around Swindon Works 'C' Shop and dump in July 1964, at least this one went with its rods on.

Plate 343.  No.1473 (w/d Aug '62)          2nd March 1963                    Fed-2

Plate 344.  No.1474 (w/d Sep '64)          12th August 1962            P.Askey - Kershaw

Whilst in steam a class that photographically eluded me, always seemingly tucked away in some inaccessible corner. No.1474 was one of the regulars on our local Greenford to Ealing Broadway push-pull service, dieselised in 1958. Our picture shows the loco stored in 1962 at the rear of Southall depot. Transferred to Gloucester, withdrawal came two years later. Sister engine No 1473 transferred to Gloucester in 1961 but was withdrawn in August 1962 where she now sits out time on the Horton Road dump which backs on to the old terrace housing along Great Western Street.

# '1361' & '1366' CLASS

Plate 345. No.1361 (w/d May '61)    15th October 1961    Kodak 44A

Plate 346. No.1368 (w/d Oct '64)    31st January 1965    Minolta SR1

The '1361s' were a small class of saddle tanks, Swindon's last, built in 1910. All withdrawn by 1962. No.1361 was one of the earlier ones to go having been withdrawn in May 1961 and cut up shortly after this misty Swindon dump photo was taken. Of the latter build '1366' class panniers, withdrawals came early in 1960 but three, including No.1368, had a few years extra life working the former Southern Railway Wenford Bridge branch until withdrawal in October 1964. Our locomotive found its way to Barry dump, but sadly even that could not save it.

# THE FINAL CUT

Plate 347. No.7035 (w/d Aug '64)    5th July 1964    Minolta SR1

Plate 348. Nos.3646(w/d May '64) & 8452 (w/d April '64)   5th July 1964    Minolta SR1

'C' shop did indeed mean the final cut for many Western engines. Built in the early 1930s 'C', or the Concentration Shed and dump, were situated on reclaimed land on the far reaches of Swindon Works bounded by the Paddington main line and the old MSWJRly. As seen in the photographs a large overhead crane was available and all facilities for cutting engines were present, despite this many locomotives were cut up on the dump itself. Scrapping steam engines finished in early 1965 but recommenced in the early 1970s on Swindon's own diesel hydraulics.

Plate 349. No.W8W (w/d Jan '59)       5th May 1961                    Kodak 44A

Plate 350. No.W21W (w/d Aug '62)      16th December 1962              Fed-2

Being a trainspotter at Southall from the mid 1950s onwards I was accustomed to the sleek GW Railcars some of which, by that time, were twenty years old. Both passenger and parcel types were allocated to Southall with the last one going in 1961. W8W was photographed outside Swindon Stock shed, withdrawn and fire damaged, and was one of the earlier AEC built streamlined versions. Swindon plant's own gas works forms a setting for withdrawn W21W, one of the latter unstreamlined Swindon built railcars and one of Southall depot's last GW railcars.

## STEAM LOCOMOTIVE DUMPS

Plate 351. Eastleigh 'Dead Row'       27th September 1964       Minolta SR1

Plate 352. Nine Elms 'Old Shed'       25th May 1963       Mamiya C22

Loco dumps in or around locomotive works and sheds such as Stratford and Swindon were common. Eastleigh shed was no exception and 'Dead Row' at the rear of the loco depot alongside Eastleigh airfield where the prototype Spitfire first flew was well known for many years. Nine Elms 'Old Shed' and yards always held withdrawn or stored engines, initially from the 1959 Eastern Section electrification to the mass withdrawals of late 1962. By my last visit in 1964 most old stock had been replaced by modern Southern types and BR Standards.

Exmouth Junction dump
June 1964

Plate 353. Feltham                    15th September 1963                    Mamiya C22

Plate 354. Feltham                    7th June 1964                    Minolta SR1

Such were the numbers of locos arriving at Nine Elms in 1959 that some elderly 4-4-0s finished up at Feltham (Plate 367), these eventually going by February 1961. However by the Summer of 1962 its own displaced 'Hump' shunters were put into store (Plates 127 and 377) and within a year or so Feltham became a collection point for withdrawn locomotives. Plate 353 shows part of the dump in September 1963 including a solitary GW pannier and an 'M7' tank. During June 1964 a scrap train is made up of withdrawn 'S15s' destined for Barry. This was apparently stopped at Staines when lead engine No.30506 failed.

Plate 355.  Branksome                    17th May 1964                    Minolta SR1

Hove dump, February 1963

Plate 356.  Hove                    18th April 1963                    P.Askey - Minolta A5

During 1963/4 I became aware of three locomotive dumps, at Exmouth Junction, Branksome and Hove. Exmouth Junction in September 1964 contained many locos but was difficult to photograph. Branksome, now closed, held 'M7' tanks comprising of Nos.30036/48/29/667/108 all withdrawn May 1964 from Bournemouth depot. Hove dump held all of Brighton's stock withdrawn at year's end 1962. On a very dirty misty day in February 1963 this dump held Nos.30901/11/15/16/23, 31891/5, 32338/41/2, and 32417/8. It was reported that these locos worked right up to the end and some into early 1963.

Plate 357.  No.35002 (w/d Feb '64)          5th April 1964          Minolta SR1

Plate 358.  No.35006 (w/d Aug '64)          27th September 1964          Minolta SR1

Whilst Old Oak Common gave way to diesel traction, sadly there was no future for Nine Elms. The total dereliction and hopelessness in the final years I missed, but the raw emotions of such times I understand when the cast iron foundry where I worked closed and a once proud plant gave way to rack and ruin. Withdrawals of the once streamlined 'Merchant Navy' class began in February 1964, two years after the first 'King', and Nos.35002/15 of Nine Elms were the first to go. August 1964 saw the next few and one of these No.35006 heads up the 'dead' sidings at Eastleigh.

# THE 'BATTLE OF BRITAINS'

Plate 359.  No.34067 (w/d Nov '63)        26th July 1964              Minolta SR1

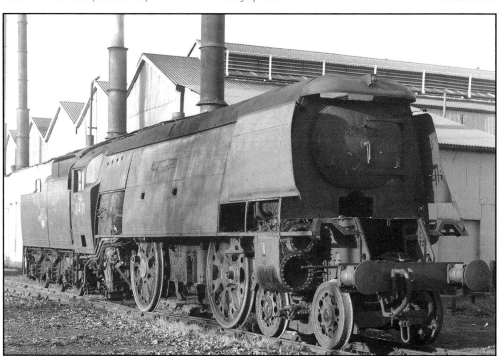

Plate 360.  No.34110 (w/d Nov '63)        29th September 1964          Minolta SR1

The Southern Railway light Pacifics were known as the 'West County' and 'Battle of Britain' classes and were originally streamlined. Most of the class were rebuilt from 1957 onwards and withdrawals commenced in 1963 with the rebuilds going in 1964. No.34067 was withdrawn in November 1963 and she sits on Eastleigh's 'dead' siding some nine months later, her nameplate and crest having been simply cut out. A fate worse than death seems to have befallen No.34110. Parked up at the rear of Eastleigh Works she appears somewhat stripped and when photographed was not even withdrawn.

# THE 'LORD NELSONS'

Plate 361.  No.30853 (w/d Feb '62)          25th March 1962          Kodak Retinette 1A

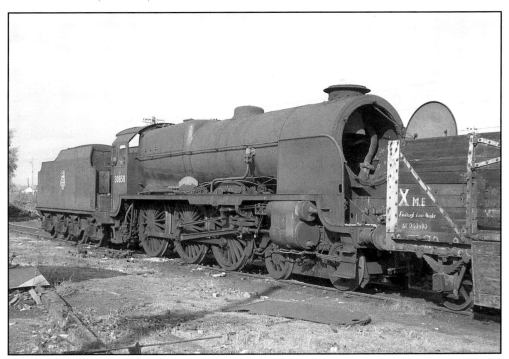

Plate 362.  No.30858 (w/d Aug '61)          29th October 1961          Kodak 44A

Built over a four year period from 1926 and for a time the most powerful locomotives in the country. Allocated to Eastleigh from 1959 onwards the first withdrawal was in May 1961 and they were rapidly dispatched. From the first one withdrawn to the last example being scrapped took a mere nineteen months. Both photographs at Eastleigh, which cut them all, No.30853 already looks in a sorry state one month after withdrawal, whilst No.30858 was the second example withdrawn and soon cut up. Note the 'Schools' class smoke deflector on the deck.

# 'S15' & 'H15' CLASS

Plate 363.  No.30515 (w/d July '63)          29th September 1963                    Mamiya C22

Plate 364.  No.30522 (w/d Oct '61)           29th October 1961                      Kodak 44A

Urie's 'S15' goods locomotives were built in 1920/21and Maunsell completed a further batch from 1927 to 1936. Mixed traffic class 'H15s' were originally built by Urie in 1905 with a further batch by Maunsell in 1924. All had detail differences. All of the 'S15s' outlasted the 'H15' which had gone by the end of 1961. Withdrawal of 'S15' commenced in late 1962 and No.30515 had been in store at Eastleigh since withdrawal in July 1963. Over at the Works, 'H15' No.30522 was withdrawn the month the photograph was taken and had only weeks to go before scrapping.

# THE 'SCHOOLS'

Plate 365.  No.30913 (w/d  Jan'62)          11th January 1962          Kodak Retinette 1A

Plate 366.  No.30923 (w/d Dec '62)          18th August 1963          Mamiya C22

The 'Schools' class were built between 1930 and 1935 and had the distinction of being the last and most powerful 4-4-0 in the country. Withdrawals commenced in February 1961 but unlike the 'Lord Nelsons' the last rusting hulk was not finally cut up until May 1964. Eastleigh Works cut up nearly half of the class and No.30913 was one of the earlier examples withdrawn, note the newly installed overhead lamps. Meanwhile, dumped around another part of the Works, some sixteen months later, was No.30923 one of the last withdrawn in December 1962 and a former resident of Hove dump.

# 'D1' & 'L1' CLASS

Plate 367.  No.31545 (w/d March '61)          December 1960          C.Featherstone - Plastic Box Thing

Plate 368.  No.31786 (w/d Feb '62)          11th February 1962          Kodak Retinette 1A

The 'D1s' were rebuilt from Class 'D' and were gone by 1961 although many were out of use at Nine Elms from 1959 onwards. However No.31545 and two others finished up stored at Feltham and were finally withdrawn and scrapped at Ashford in March 1961. The Class 'E1s' were identical, the last three were still active at Stewarts Lane and Bricklayers Arms in March 1961, but had also gone by year's end. Class 'L1' were new engines in 1927 and like the others had gone by 1961 except No.31786 wnich was active on light freight and parcel work right up to withdrawal in February 1962.

Plate 369. Nos.31621 & 31624 (w/d June '64)     9th August 1964     Minolta SR1

Plate 370. No.31852 (w/d Sept '63)     10th November 1963     Mamiya C22

The original Mogul was SECR ‘N’ class No.31810 built in 1917, with the remainder from 1920 through to 1932. The origins of the ‘U’ class were rebuilds of the ‘River’ class 2-6-4T built in 1917 and rebuilt as Moguls in 1927 with additional locomotives built up to 1931. Withdrawals commenced in 1962, the bulk going in 1964 and the last few hanging on until 1966. New build ‘U’ class Nos.31624 and 31621 are stored outside Nine Elms ‘Old Shed’ having been withdrawn in June 1964 whilst ‘N’ No.31852, withdrawn in September 1963, from Redhill lies dead at Eastleigh.

Plate 371. No.31877 (w/d Oct '62)　　　25th August 1963　　　Mamiya C22

Plate 372. No.31879 (w/d Oct'62)　　　25th May 1963　　　Mamiya C22

The 'N1'and 'U1' were three cylinder versions of the two cylinder classes 'N' and 'U', and, as such, there were considerable differences in front end design. Both classes suffered wholesale withdrawal in December 1962 with a handful of 'U1s' going on until the Summer of 1963. Both photographs are of 'N1s', No.31877 is partially cut up at Eastleigh Works by August 1963 and No.31879 is still in store at Stewarts Lane but will be scrapped by December 1963. Several locomotives of both classes managed to avoid the cutter's torch until May 1964.

# 'K' CLASS

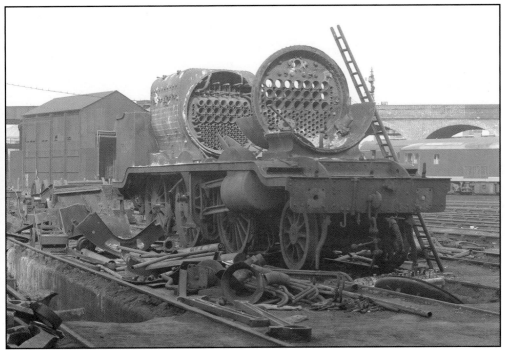

Plate 373.  No.32347 (w/d Dec '62)          13th October 1963          Mamiya C22

Plate 374.  No.32341 (w/d Dec '62)          18th August 1963          Mamiya C22

Built between 1913 and 1921 these LBSCR locomotives gave sterling service right up to withdrawal in December 1962 many having received major repairs and were in excellent order. Many were stored during 1963 with Nos.32337/40/3/7 noted at Stewarts Lane, 32338/41/2 at Hove and 32345/53 at Three Bridges. No.32347 was actually scrapped at Stewarts Lane in October 1963 with the last of the stored locos there going by June 1964. Eastleigh Works has set-to cutting up No.32341 by August 1963 but one lingered on until October 1964.

# '700' CLASS

Plate 375. No.30350 (w/d March '62)        25th March 1962        Kodak Retinette 1A

Plate 376. No.30368 (w/d Dec '62)        29th September 1963        Mamiya C22

By my standards the Class '700s' were old locomotives built in 1897 for the LSWR by Dübs & Co, Glasgow. with similar locos supplied to the North British and Caledonian Railways. They were rebuilt by the Southern Railway in the 1920s and withdrawals commenced in 1957. The last one to leave the London area was No.30346 (Plate 126) stored at Feltham by August 1962 with the last seven going in December 1962. No.30368, as seen at Eastleigh, being one of those. Not much remains of No.30350 at Eastleigh in March 1962, but a few actually survived into 1964 before scrapping.

Plate 377. No.30520 (w/d Nov '62)    21st July 1963    Mamiya C22

Plate 378. No.30582 (w/d July '61)    29th October 1961    Kodak 44A

Two classes of large tank locomotives, classified 'G16' and 'H16', were built in 1921 by the LSWR for working the large marshalling yards at Feltham. All were withdrawn at the end of 1962 and No.30520, an 'H16', is by July 1963 dumped at the end of Feltham's long headshunt. No.30582 was one of three survivors of a large class, latterly known as '0415' which worked the Lyme Regis branch until replaced by Ivatt tanks. All three were withdrawn in 1961 and No.30582 was caught dead at Eastleigh prior to scrapping in March 1962.

Plate 379. Nos.31518 (w/d Jan '64) & 31263 (w/d Jan '64)    2nd August 1964    Minolta SR1

Plate 380. No.32635 (w/d March '63)    10th February 1963    Fed-2

'H' class built by the SECR between 1904 and 1915. Withdrawals commenced in 1955 and Nos.31518 and 31263 worked the Three Bridges to East Grinstead push & pull until steam finished in January 1964. Stored at Three Bridges until hauled away for scrap in late 1964. No.32635 was one of the LBSCR ' Terrier' tanks. Originally No.DS377 the Brighton Works shunter and painted in LBSCR colours. Withdrawn in March 1963 it apparently had already lost its funnel to preserved 'A1' No.DS680. Brighton depot's last 'A1X' was coal stage pilot No.32678. It went in October 1963.

# 'O2' & 'G6' CLASS

Plates 381 'O2' class No.30183 and 'G6' class No.30277    29th October 1961    Kodak44A

Class 'O2' 0-4-4 tank, a class which gained fame on the Isle of Wight and remained in service there until 1967. Their classmates on the mainland did not have such a charmed life and our photo shows withdrawn No.30183 on Eastleigh Works, the last two going in December 1962. Class 'G6' 0-6-0 tank No.30277 was the last remaining example in BR revenue stock being withdrawn and scrapped in November 1961. One other, in departmental stock, lasted until 1962.

# TAIL PIECE

Plate 382                    12th July 1964                P Wells - Kodak 44A

The cut up remains of 'M7' tank No.30104. The bunker seems to have found a home under a Gresley carriage bogie at R S Hayes yard, Bridgend. According to records it was withdrawn in May 1961 and scrapped the following month. Obviously some bits linger longer.

## INTERNAL COMBUSTION

Plate 383. Petrol engine    19th July 1964    Minolta SR1

Plate 384. Petrol engine    6th September 1964    Minolta SR1

It is to my greatest regret that the industrial, as well as a lot of other things, passed me by. Whilst trainspotting with Buster in the mid 1950s we became aware of the beautiful little green outside cylinder saddle tanks of Southall and Kensal Green gas works. Sadly their numbers meant nothing in the Ian Allan ABCs and that was that. The top picture is a little Planet diesel shunting wagons alongside Kensal Green Gas Works whilst the other is an unidentified 0-4-0 petrol or diesel shunter working alongside the Paddington main line near Hayes, Middlesex.

Plate 385.  Diesel shunter                    12th July 1964                    Minolta SR1

Plate 386.  Diesel shunter                    6th September 1964                    Minolta SR1

Featured here are two larger types of 0-4-0 diesel shunters. Photographed in July 1964 is the R S Hayes, Bridgend, scrap yard shunter used for moving dead locomotives around their yard. It was reported in the railway press that ex-GWR 0-4-0ST No.1151 was shunting this yard in November 1964. The other diesel shunter, named *Churchill*, and built by Fowlers, was photographed from a train coming into Newbury in September 1964. Sadly no other details, other than the wagons being shunted are designated 'non pool' and are for internal use only.

Plate 387.  Ex-GW No.1151  0-4-0ST                    12th July 1964                    Minolta SR1

Plate 388.  *Gordon*  0-4-0ST                    12th July 1964                    Minolta SR1

My nineteenth birthday present, 12th July 1964, and a trip to Llanelly with a surprise visit to R S Hayes scrap yard, because we did not know it existed until passing it on the train. We got there by bus, yes a country bus on a Sunday. The scrap yard was set down from the main line and on hearing a 'poop-poop' we climbed up the embankment and found No.1151, withdrawn August 1963, on a scrap train by a closed railway station opposite the yard. A private loco on BR tracks? On the other hand poor old *Gordon*, and not quite *Gordon* the big engine, has had its last gasp.

Plate 389. 0-6-0ST           3rd March 1963           Fed-2

Plate 390. Austerity 0-6-0ST         3rd March 1963         Fed-2

Llantrisant, South Wales, March 1963. Three saddle tanks Nos.16, 17, and 22 stored alongside the main line near to the loco depot. Nos.16 and 22 are War Department saddle tanks whilst No.17 is a Hunslet. In one photo, not printed, a gas works hoves in the background. Any takers?

Plate 391. *Abernethy* 0-4-0ST        12th July 1964        P.Wells - Kodak 44A

Plate 392. Austerity 0-6-0ST        31st January 1965        P.Wells - Halina

Like *Gordon*, another little saddle tank at R S Hayes yard, *Aberneathy,* awaits the same fate. Unlike their larger BR counterparts these little work horses, often with a lifetime of work behind them, meet the same fate with little or no interest. Longmoor Military Railway 'WD' 0-6-0 saddle tanks Nos.106, 108, 109, 130, 178 and 203 were noted on Barry dump during January 1965. No.203 hit the headlines whilst being transported to Barry when its low loader became jammed on a hump bridge near Newbury and caused chaos for several hours in July 1963.

Two old locomotive tenders photographed at Eastleigh Works in October 1961. The Southern example numbered 422 from a Class 'L12' 4-4-0 withdrawn in 1951 and in use, or was in use, holding diesel fuel oil. The two LMS tenders were in crimson red and rust and could have been converted for use during the locomotive oil fired trials of the late 1940s.

Swindon's mysterious wooden tender.
What think you? Lived for years behind the stock shed.
Want to know more? Easy. Buy yourself *The Railway Magazine*, May 1964 and all will be revealed.

On the left 4-wheeler, DW108, is one of the last 4-wheelers built, probably in 1895. It is a five compartment 3rd, 28ft. long. Possibly it is one which worked miners' services into BR days in South Wales, prior being to be transferred into Departmental service at Aberdare where it was photographed on 20th August 1961.

The other, is No.14198, a very late clerestory one of 40 built 1903-4, eight compartment 3rds for branch line work, 46ft 6in long, again quite possibly one of the few which survived in South Wales in passenger service into the very early 1950s and then stayed there in Departmental stock, photographed in the Newport area on 12th July 1964.

# LAST ORDERS

Ted in his Rocker period 1965!

By 1965 railways and all that went with them were on the backburner. During 1964 motorbikes had taken us over and our odd assortment of lightweight machines had matured into adult size versions. Peter and Paul had gone the way of the Japanese with 305cc Hondas complete with electric starters while I had gravitated to a Clubmans 500cc BSA Gold Star and John and the others to Velocettes. We had also undergone a sixties image change, leather jackets etc and thus found ourselves not welcome in polite society. West London's transport caffs such as the Ace Café or the Busy Bee were our new home, we had become in the terminology of the time - Rockers.

White van man had allowed me the pleasure of driving into him shortly before Christmas, so on a visit to Old Oak Common, Willesden and Southall with Peter and Paul on the 24th January 1965 I was relegated to being a passenger.

The demolition of Old Oak was advanced by this stage, a sizeable chunk of the loco shed had gone with one of the four turntables cleared and the framework for the three road diesel fuelling depot well advanced on the site. Trackwork had been cleared and the south side of the coaler was out of use. Forty diesels were scattered around the shed site, and even on this date there was a good mix of Western Region diesel hydraulics to Sulzer diesel electrics. Steam still managed a respectable thirty including two 'Castles' and four 'Halls', mostly without nameplates. Even the two stationary boilers were finally cold and awaiting the scrap man's torch. Old Oak finally closed to steam two months later.

Old Oak Common

8F on breakdown train, Willesden

Following the closure of Camden and Neasden, Willesden's short lived glory days of 'Coronations' and 'Britannias' had gone. Thirty nine unkempt steam locos, namely 'Black 5s', '8Fs', large tanks and numerous Standard '78xxx' 2-6-0s, shared with forty two diesels mainly, in 'TOPS speak', of classes '20', '24' and '40'. Like Old Oak, Willesden's days were numbered the shed closing within nine months.

Travelling on to Southall the loco shed was still steeped in the past, with forty nine grimy hulks in attendance, diesels being limited to a few shunters. Classes '28xx', '61xx' and Standard '9Fs' being well represented including a very woebegone 'Castle'. The huge loco dumps that had characterised Old Oak and Southall in recent years had been cleared, but at the time of our visit to Southall nine locos remained including four '45xx' light Prairie tanks. Southall closed to steam by the end of the year.

The last two trips of 1965 with a camera were with Paul. We had planned a trip to Barry dump and went on the 31st January, the first of what was to become a yearly pilgrimage. However, the weather was so cold we dressed in bike gear but went by train.

It proved pointless stopping off at Slough and Reading, both loco sheds were devoid of any steam with only a handful of diesel shunters at home. Travelling past Gloucester, the loco shed seemed active enough with mainly Midland engines in the yards. At Severn Tunnel Junction a

Southall

huge dump of withdrawn locos had collected, no doubt destined for the scrap yards of South Wales. On arrival at Barry a quick visit to the old steam shed found ten diesels, mainly class '37s', but interestingly former GW shunters Nos.15101/2/3. The dump itself held 108 assorted types mainly ex-GW, including one small pannier No.1368 which sadly did not survive. Southern classes were appearing as were the two SDJR '7Fs' and seven Longmore Military Railway 'WD' saddle tanks, two of which were already being broken up. The trip turned out to be a photographic disaster, on processing the films with a new developer, mine came out somewhat thin so Paul's got the advantage of an extra minute . . .

Barry dump

The last trip was to Guildford, Salisbury and Eastleigh on the 7th February and as I was still bikeless rode pillion on Paul's Honda. We must have been keen, the weather was dreadful, dull, mist and rain. Guildford contained twenty steam and a few diesels. The shed pilot was the usual 'USA' tank, the bulk of the remainder being 'U's or 'N's. No photos taken here. Salisbury managed a meagre twenty one steam the only Southern types being light Pacifics, the rest being BR Standards. Eight diesels, including three 'Warships', contributed to the misery. No photos here either, you have to be determined to photograph in sheeting rain.

The ride from Salisbury to Eastleigh had its highlights, Paul had the ignomy of being overtaken by a car, an Austin Healy 3000, the proper job. I must have had total faith in Paul's riding abilities to go chasing cars in the pouring rain. It was, in the slang of the time, a 'right little burn-up'! However, we had the better of him and arrived at Eastleigh somewhat the sooner.

Dull and miserable it was, so were we and so was Eastleigh, but at least the rain had eased off. The loco yards resembled Barry, 109 locos on shed and it was a job to sort out which ones were going on and which ones never were, dead locos being scattered all over the place. Southern types totalled forty two, mainly Pacifics not that they looked that way. Standard types ruled the roost

No.34079 at Eastleigh

but interestingly twenty one Midland types were mixed in with a very dead 'Jubilee'. Eastleigh had a very cosmopolitan air about it in stark contrast to a few years previous. We watched flat top No.34079 steam off shed into the mist and rain, and that was that. Not surprisingly the films came as uninspired as the day itself, not a good end to one's photographic endeavours.

About a month later I met up with Buster again, his motorcycling days over when being overtaken by his own sidecar wheel. He now drove a battered Austin A55 van with little in the way of suspension. He was keen on motorbike road racing and it wasn't long before we were bouncing our way to Brands Hatch racetrack. Watching all the frantic activity in the paddock I knew then and there I wanted to be on the inside of the fence. My enthusiasm even took me as far as a session with a racing school and for my twenty five pounds, not a small sum in those days, I received a detailed report stating that 'this man shows promise'. I bet we all did at that price.

Looking back being a leather jacketed anti-social hooligan lasted shorter than being a trainspotter, the bikes were eventually traded in for rusty Vauxhalls and Fords and the leather jackets and transport cafés gave way to suits and dancehalls

By the end of 1967 I had met my Iris at said dancehall, Greenfords very own 'Oldfield', and by the Summer of 1968 had persuaded her to go on a day's excursion to Barry Island, she thought the South Wales equivalent to Southend or Brighton. Oh how wrong she was.

But all that's another story, the railway negatives of the early '60s were already asleep and would stay that way for another forty years or so.

Iris - the things a girl will do!

# AND FINALLY . . . SPOTTERS NO MORE!

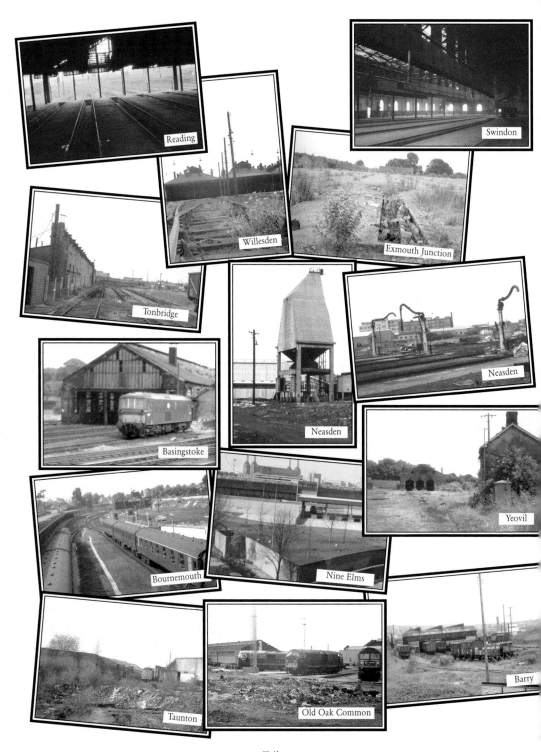

Reading

Swindon

Willesden

Exmouth Junction

Tonbridge

Neasden

Basingstoke

Neasden

Yeovil

Bournemouth

Nine Elms

Taunton

Old Oak Common

Barry

Tail note:
To the wonderful ladies on the checkouts at the old Somerfield store, Chard.
You were right, men can only do only one thing at any one time!